YOUTH, CRIME AND POLICE WORK

Youth, Crime and Police Work

Maggy Lee
Lecturer
Department of Sociology
University of Essex

First published in Great Britain 1998 by
MACMILLAN PRESS LTD
Houndmills, Basingstoke, Hampshire RG21 6XS and London
Companies and representatives throughout the world

A catalogue record for this book is available from the British Library.

ISBN 0–333–66670–4

First published in the United States of America 1998 by
ST. MARTIN'S PRESS, INC.,
Scholarly and Reference Division,
175 Fifth Avenue, New York, N.Y. 10010

ISBN 0–312–17762–3

Library of Congress Cataloging-in-Publication Data
Lee, Maggy.
Youth, crime, and police work / Maggy Lee.
p.   cm.
Includes bibliographical references and index.
ISBN 0–312–17762–3 (cloth)
1. Juvenile delinquency—Great Britain—Prevention. 2. Pre-trial
intervention—Great Britain.   3. Police services for juveniles–
–Great Britain.   4. Social work with juvenile delinquents—Great
Britain.   I. Title.
HV9145.A5L44 1997
364.36'0941—dc21   97–26515
                                                        CIP

This book is printed on paper suitable for recycling and made from fully managed and
sustained forest sources.

10   9   8   7   6   5   4   3   2   1
07   06   05   04   03   02   01   00   99   98

Printed in Great Britain by
The Ipswich Book Company Ltd
Ipswich, Suffolk

Contents

List of Figures

List of Tables

Acknowledgements

Many people have helped me through the process of writing this book. My apologies that so few of them are named individually here, but my thanks to them all.

I am grateful to all those in the police force areas, social services, probation services and education welfare services, magistrates, young people and their parents, who agreed to be interviewed and facilitated the fieldwork on which this book is based.

Thanks to Loraine Gelsthorpe and Allison Morris for supervising the original MPhil and PhD theses, Eugene McLaughlin for his criticial insights into policing and encouragement over the last ten years, my old colleagues at ISDD and new ones at Essex University for providing an environment of scholarship. Denis Jones offered valuable criticism of an earlier version of the book but, as always, should not be blamed for my errors. Thanks too to Chris Ellis for helping me put my work in perspective.

The source of Figures 1.1 and 2.1 and Table 2.1 is Crown copyright. The author and publisher would also like to thank the University of Wales Press (Cardiff) for permission to reproduce in Chapter 6 material which appeared in an earlier form in L. Noaks, M. Levi and M. Maguire (eds) *Contemporary Issues in Criminology* (1995).

Abbreviations

ACMD	Advisory Council on the Misuse of Drugs
ACPO	Association of Chief Police Officers
CPS	Crown Prosecution Service
CYPA	Children and Young Persons Act
IT	Intermediate Treatment
JJB	Juvenile Justice Bureau
JLB	Juvenile Liaison Bureau
JLP	Juvenile Liaison Panel

Introduction

In May 1994, a police constable, Steve Guscott from the Somerset and Avon Constabulary, was brought before the magistrates' court and pleaded guilty to common assault. He was alleged by the prosecution to have clipped the ear of a 14-year-old boy. The events seemed ordinary enough:

> A gang of teenagers had been banging on the pensioners' front door and kicking the cat flap. They shouted abuse and ran away when the officer approached them. Later that evening when PC Guscott came across one of the group in an unlit alleyway – the 14-year-old boy – he grabbed him and slapped him on the cheek with his open hand. The boy, according to the prosecution, suffered a nose bleed.
>
> (*Independent*, 15 June 1994)

PC Guscott was fined £100 and ordered to pay £50 in compensation to the juvenile. What followed was an extraordinary degree of public approbation of the constable's behaviour, criticism of the court ruling, and even offers to pay his fine. The *Star*, *Sun* and *Mirror* newspapers were reportedly inundated with some 64 000 telephone calls declaring their support for the constable and concern that he was being punished for using 'good, old-fashioned police methods'.[1] In a phone-in poll conducted over a period of about two hours by an early morning television programme, 98 per cent of nearly 72 000 respondents said that PC Guscott was right to do what he had done.[2] According to police sources, over 16 000 local people signed a petition backing the constable as he was subsequently reprimanded by his chief constable in an internal disciplinary hearing.[3] Many sighed for the days of their youth when every constable gave the erring young 'a clip round the ear'. As the then Prime Minister called for a 'real national effort to build an "anti-yob culture"' in his speech about changing the climate against crime, the general message is that society should not allow 'youngsters to slip further into bad habits by condoning or repeatedly cautioning their offences'.[4]

For the police, the problem is not so much the increase in youth crime *per se*, but that their hands are tied in the fight against crime. As one Police Federation representative put it, 'officers faced a moral dilemma because the courts were incapable of dealing with such unruly behaviour'.[5] The prosecution of the officer in this case arguably sends 'the wrong message to "teenage hooligans" that they can behave in an unacceptable way and that the police can do nothing – in the absence of an arrest – to control it' (McKenzie, 1995, p.198). It is now commonplace for the police to complain that their efforts are constantly frustrated by a system 'weighted in favour of the criminal' – court delays, 'no comment' interviews, rules of disclosure that force prosecutions to be abandoned, a Crown Prosecution Service too eager to drop charges on cost grounds, and a bureaucratic system incapable of delivering speedy justice.

Away from the publicity surrounding the Guscott case, the incident only highlights the distinctive police capacity to use force in the enforcement of laws and order maintenance – that is, as specialists in coercion. This does not mean, of course, that the police routinely invoke their legal powers to resolve conflicts. Significantly, the unique dimension of police authority is most potent precisely when the police decide *not* to enforce the law but to resort to other informal means of discipline.

This book is about the policing and punishment of young people outside the formal court system in England and Wales. It describes and analyses how, and with what effects, police discretionary powers have been exercised in relation to young people in the historical and contemporary contexts. Chapter 1 begins with a discussion of the way in which police–youth interaction was constructed historically. The police had responsibilities for surveilling the lives of children and young people in ways that extended well beyond the notion of criminal offence or its prevention. Police policies and concerns, which were much more interventionist than those considered acceptable for most adults, were developed in the context of controlling and monitoring the social life of young people. In particular, the traditional mandate that the police had in controlling the 'street residents' and their activities, and the wide discretionary powers available under street offences and vagrancy acts, meant that many young people were routinely moved on, stopped and searched, or 'told off' by the police.

Against the wider development of an interventionist strategy in governing the lives of deprived and depraved children throughout the nineteenth and twentieth centuries, the police gradually acquired an increased, yet sometimes ambiguous, mandate to intervene in the family. In 1883 a police constable from Worcestershire was reprimanded for 'improperly acceding to the request of a Mr Hollis, to give his son a beating for staying away from school and sleeping out nights' (Emsley, 1991, p.75). Such an incident stands on the boundary of public and private domains which the policing of delinquents constantly straddled during this period. Elsewhere, police work in the service role as welfare agents and moral guardians, catching truants and tracking down missing children, constituted important occasions of police involvement with young people. Backed by early quasi-sociological and psychological theories of criminogenic environment and defective discipline, juvenile liaison strategies permitted police officers to intervene at an early stage in the assumed development of criminal careers – for instance, through home visits, liaison with schools, informal (and later formal) cautions, and supervision of girls drifting into a life of immorality. Club work was seen to have a strong impact on local delinquency figures, as many juvenile offenders were reprimanded at a police station and encouraged to join police-run clubs rather than being taken to the juvenile court (Weinberger, 1995). But the balance between the use of police discretion with regard to juvenile delinquents and their role as law enforcers remained an uneasy one. The history of juvenile policing thus requires an historical understanding of the shifting relations between these two aspects of police work.

Over time, police discretion and specialized service functions have become synthesized within the framework of 'diversion' in youth justice reform. As the second chapter argues, the concept of diversion has shown a capacity to embrace a number of imperatives across the political spectrum. With the rise of what some commentators have termed the 'new penology' (Feeley and Simon, 1992; see also Garland, 1996), diversion is best understood in terms of the management of unruly groups and the state's adaptation to high crime rates and high case loads. The goal is not so much to eliminate crime but to limit the level of demand placed upon the criminal justice system by letting minor offences and offenders fall below the threshold of official notice. The police caution is now the predominant means of disposing of low-risk delinquents for whom the more formal court intervention is judged too expensive or unnecessary: three out of five young offenders identified by the police are cautioned rather than prosecuted in England and Wales (Audit Commission, 1996). The question is whether the Home Office's initiatives to set clear policy objectives and promote internal rationality in case disposal can bring about police decisions which are impartial, more consistent with official purposes of cautioning, and open to police managers and other agencies. Chapter 2 reviews the existing research evidence and concludes that, as the ideology of the police original powers continues to locate police cautioning firmly outside statutory control, the impact of managerialist initiatives on controlling police discretion has been far from totalizing.

The next four chapters look at the key features of the administrative processing of juvenile delinquents outside the court system, the organization of case disposal in four multi-agency settings, and the impact of this managerialist approach on young people and their families. A key strand to crime control that emerged in the 1980s took the form of multi-agency cooperation. Chapter 3 contrasts the power of appeals to the multi-agency consultative approach with the local organization of juvenile delinquency. Under the multi-agency approach, many caution decisions were made not by the police alone but in consultation with social agencies behind closed doors. In principle, this shift from 'judicial' to 'administrative' justice should have enhanced the expert status of the social agencies participating in such initiatives. In reality, the agendas of those agencies with a core law and order mandate were prioritized at the expense of others even during the heyday of diversion in the early 1990s.

Chapters 4 and 5 highlight the problematic nature of the multi-agency approach to crime management by examining the basis for the selective processing of juvenile delinquents. To the extent that the police control the flow of information to other agencies, the case for caution can be regarded as a police construct. So why are some young people dealt with outside the formal court system and not others? The key point is that case disposals depend not so much upon the nature of the offence but on the exigencies of agencies' practice and technocratic considerations of the pre-court apparatus. As we shall see, the multi-agency forum can best be described as a site where various agents, differing in their bargaining power and working assumptions about juvenile delinquency, come into interaction and seek to identify and manage the 'cooperative' and least intractable groups efficiently. The multi-agency conflicts that this sifting process generate further illustrate the complex nature of the partnership approach to crime control.

According to the official rhetoric, cautioning can be seen as an alternative to court-based punishment. There is also an implicit assumption that informal handling of delinquents (as in the Scottish Children Hearings System) can promote a sense of partnership between the state and the parents of offending children. Chapter 6 examines the extent to which these viewpoints are commensurate with the experience of those juveniles and parents on the receiving-end of cautioning. The final chapter reflects upon the many facets of the policing of young people and considers the more general lessons that can be learned from this study of police cautioning as part of a strategy to regulate the caseloads of the criminal justice system.

The empirical research on which this book is based took place in four police force divisions in south-east England between 1990 and 1992, when multi-agency consultation was a central plank of national policy in cautioning. Semi-structured interviews were conducted with police officers, probation officers, social workers, education welfare officers, juvenile court magistrates, parents, and juveniles who received a police caution. I observed police cautioning sessions and multi-agency forums at work and examined all the relevant case files and policy guidelines (see Appendix). In the construction of this text, I have attempted at all times to protect the anonymity of all those who trusted me with sensitive material and information.

1 The Policing of Juvenile Delinquency

Contemporary studies of policing have emphasized the importance in police work of duties unrelated to crime detection and the arrest of offenders (Audit Commission, 1993; Cain, 1973; McLaughlin, 1996). The policing of young people exemplifies this aspect of police work. This can be illustrated by tracing the historical and ideological context within which police remedies for juvenile delinquency were developed throughout the nineteenth and twentieth centuries. So under what conditions did police come into contact with young people and what did they do in those contacts?

Not all juvenile delinquents were processed into the criminal justice system. Some form of police warning was in use in lieu of prosecution and existed in the records of the Metropolitan Police Force as early as 1833 (Steer, 1970). Informal policing, involving identification of the child and direct chastisement or a stern 'telling off' at the street level where police discretion was wider than usual, was undoubtedly frequent. The eighteenth-century definition of 'police' also meant the preservation of general welfare, especially of those ancient concerns governments had about cities: supplying them with food, controlling nuisances, and preserving the general health of the city. Even as the meaning of the word 'police' narrowed, a range of 'service' functions were taken on by the police institution directed at 'troublesome' juveniles and those considered 'at risk'.[1] Involvement in juvenile welfare and the processing of delinquents or uncontrollable children thus constituted important occasions of police involvement with young people. But the police mandate for intervention in the social lives of young people has not been an unambiguous one. Doubts over the relevance of police service work was strong within the police and outside, especially when it was seen to encroach on the jurisdiction of the court and other local state apparatus concerned with children in trouble.

The history of juvenile delinquency as a contested site for state intervention thus requires an understanding of the shifting relations between the enforcement and service role of the police.

JUVENILE DELINQUENCY AS A DISTINCT PROBLEM

In the eighteenth century juvenile offenders were tried before the same courts as adults. They were confined in the same prisons, and subjected to the same range of sentences. Those under seven were exempt from prosecution, and those between seven and fourteen were sometimes able to claim similar immunity under the principle of *doli incapax*, but in general the criminal law made no formal provision for the separate treatment of juveniles. Most historians agree that a radical transformation took place in the nineteenth century, which led to the creation of 'juvenile delinquency' as a separate and urgent problem (May, 1973; Gillis, 1975; Hewitt and Pinchbeck, 1973). But because no systematic statistics were published before the 1830s on the number of juveniles coming before the courts or on the ways they were dealt with, we still do not know precisely why, when and how juvenile delinquency came to be perceived as a major social problem. Based on their recent detailed research into the records of the Old Bailey between the early 1790s and the early 1820s, King and Noel (1993) found that the proportion of the accused under seventeen rose from 7 to 16 per cent, representing nearly a fourfold increase in absolute numbers. They suggested that the rapid rise of juvenile prosecutions in this period may be related to the changing attitudes and action of victims, magistrates, and policing agencies. In particular, changes such as the declining use of capital punishment, the growth of the idea that imprisonment could reform the young, and the ending of the practice of holding out rewards for the apprehension of criminals in proportion to the seriousness of the offence, could have led to a greater willingness of victims and prosecutors to bring juveniles to court. The resulting growth of juvenile prosecutions between 1790 and 1820 and the investigations into the problem of delinquency, notably the influential 1816 Committee for Investigating the Alarming Increase in Juvenile Delinquency in the Metropolis, seemed to cast doubt on the notion of 'juvenile delinquency' as a 'Victorian creation' (King and Noel, 1993).

A crucial feature of the recurring debate about juvenile delinquency is the paradoxical role of the family both as a primary source of delinquent behaviour and as offering the potential for its management. This form of analysis was central to the work of Mary Carpenter, a key figure in juvenile justice reform in nineteenth-century Britain, who viewed the underlying cause of delinquency as moral destitution resulting from parental neglect. But the main concern of the reformers was more with regulating the children of the poor than it was with containing the delinquent excesses of the offspring of the rich. Thus, industrial schools for children in need of care were aimed at diverting the 'perishing' classes from vice, and bringing them back to their 'true station in life' (Carpenter, 1851).[2] Equally, the reclaiming of children from the errors of their parents' ways was to be achieved by the birth of the 'child-saving movement' (cf. Platt, 1969), involving public discussion about morals and the regulation of illicit pleasures, family responsibilities and child neglect, and the links between compulsory schooling and socio-economic order. In this respect nineteenth-century juvenile justice, welfare, education and factory legislations were significant in altering the traditional 'property rights' of parents over their children, in favour of closer state surveillance, monitoring and control.

The changing relations between the state, law and family also reflected widespread social concerns and tensions at the time. In the late nineteenth century, amidst the emergence of the boy labour market and the apparent threats to the British empire (such as the Boer War), concern was expressed about a supposed 'deterioration of our race' in physical, mental and moral terms (cf. Pearson, 1983; Rose, 1990). Against a background of alarmist fears of a 'criminal class' – uncivilized, unchristian, heathen, drunken, Chartist and politically threatening – concentrated in the lowest quarters of the fast-growing urban cities, child-savers sought to catch the young recruits of a 'problem population', to maintain a disciplined workforce, and to divert the potential delinquents from a progressive career of crime.[3] As Houghton (1957, p.246) wrote, 'philanthropy and legislation might also serve the cause of social order and lessen the threat of revolution'. Accordingly, the removal of these children from the streets offered a synthesis of altruism and self-protection for the propertied classes: kindness could nip crime in the bud.[4]

This does not mean that families were always passive recipients of state intervention. Working-class parents, both casual labourers and artisans, also invoked the custodial powers of the law when, according to their own perceptions rather than those of the state, they could either no longer maintain family discipline or else support their offspring. Jennifer Davis's (1989a) study of prosecutions by the working class in late nineteenth-century London suggests that there is evidence that working-class parents made use of the Juvenile Offenders Act to place their children in reformatories[5]:

> A warehouse worker, earning 27s. [shillings] a week, pressed a reluctant newsagent to charge his son with theft because 'his conduct had been so bad he believed he was beyond redemption'. The prosecutor himself had been content to give 'the boy a good hiding and send him home'. Other parents used theft prosecutions to have their children committed to reformatories because, having married again, they were no longer either willing or able to care for the offspring of their first marriages.   (Davis, 1989a, p.416.)

By the 1860s, the demand from parents to have children sent away was arguably so high that magistrates sought to discourage the practice by assessing parents up to 5s. a week for their children's keep (Davis, 1989a). It was feared that, as the magistrates in Surrey and Gloucestershire argued, the reformatory system 'would hold out a strong inducement for parents to encourage their children to qualify themselves for admission by repeated offences'.[6] Regulation of the lower classes had to be achieved through alternative means.

POLICE AS DOMESTIC MISSIONARY

Pivotal to the state's attempt to impose a certain social discipline on the lower classes in their everyday activities were the police. The principal arguments put forward in parliament for the creation of the Metropolitan Police, the first of the new police forces in 1829, were that it would be valuable in helping to prevent crime.[7] But with increased anxieties about fast-growing cities and slums full of poor, anonymous and potentially 'dangerous classes', there was a gradual extension of the powers of the new police to regulate city life. The new police came to represent what Petrow (1994) described as 'the penetration and continual presence of central authority throughout daily life'. The legislation which framed policework stemmed from bourgeois moral entrepreneurs and focused on readily visible proclivities. Pellew's (1982) study of the Home Office, the department of state controlling the new police, shows how bureaucratic ideals, intermingled with public officials' entrenched Conservative commitment to preserving 'the social order', influenced the work of this important department, which, more than any other, was responsible for coping with the problems generated by industrialization and urbanization. In particular, the increasing duties of its criminal department reflected the wider use of the criminal law to regulate, marginalize or suppress social behaviour of various categories which seemed to threaten order and morality.

Not every section of society was affected in the same way, however. A variety of new legislative powers, by-laws and regulations tended to direct police attention to particular social groups. Thus, ballad singers and costermongers were routinely 'moved on' – men on the tramp and seasonal workers suspected of being criminals because they were on the roads. Young women were stopped and questioned on suspicion of being prostitutes. The police were often called upon to enforce a law which favoured one particular social group – for example, enforcing the eviction of tenants under the Small Tenements Recovery Act (1838), enforcing the masters' terms of employment, and maintaining order at workers' demonstrations. Enforcing the new statutes meant that policing increasingly impinged upon the lives of what Gatrell (1980, p.335) described as 'the 30 per cent or more at the base of the social pyramid'. The statutes over vagrancy, street trading and hawking were targeted, even if indirectly, at the street economy. As a result, the poorer sections of the working class 'were forced to turn to other illegal activities to compensate for their dispossessed earnings and to supplement the family budget' (Muncie, 1986, p.20).

The creation of the new police in a district invariably led to an increase in the number of arrests for petty offences and misdemeanours under the Police Act and the Vagrancy Act, especially drunkenness and disorderly behaviour. Out of a total of 12 147 arrests reported by the Chief Constable of Greater Manchester in his report for 1843, no less than 4198 were for drunkenness, 843 for disorderly prostitutes, and 725 for 'breach of the peace' (Emsley, 1983, p.121). It was in those poor working-class districts that persons were to be found indulging in the boisterous customs, recreations and pastimes which so offended Victorian sensibilities and which the police were directed to control. 'The police came as unwelcome spectators into the very nexus of urban neighbourhood life', in the words of Robert Storch (1975, p.84). If the beat-patrol system was not geared to coping with extraordinary disorder, it was ideal for coping with minor infringements. Individual policemen could be relied upon to sort out traffic jams, order blockages removed from the public footpath, break up pub brawls and help landlords evict tenants. The imposition of a new level of order was also central to the behaviour of the rural constabularies: a General Memorandum from the police chief of the Huntingdonshire force to his men emphasized routine policing on order and suspect groups – for instance, 'travelling hawkers', 'tramps', 'gypsies and others driving without reins' (Emsley, 1991, pp.71–2).

THE POLICING OPTIONS

Not all laws were relentlessly enforced by the police, however. Sometimes this was due to inadequate numbers. In slums, where the police lacked sufficient manpower to suppress disorder, they allowed law-breaking behaviour to go on which they would have suppressed elsewhere. According to Davis's study (1989b) of policing of the notorious Jennings Buildings in Kensington in the late nineteenth century, a pattern which was soon reproduced in slums all over London, the police turned a blind eye to clearly law-breaking behaviour such as fights inside the Buildings. At the same time, the police concentrated their limited resources upon controlling the Buildings' residents on the streets and arresting them for loitering, drunkenness, and other police-defined offences. The constraints placed upon their need for public finance meant that the police were unable to operate without a substantial amount of public acquiescence. Sometimes public order was better secured by non-interference, as in the case of fairs and Sunday trading (Miller, 1977; Smith, 1985). Some of the early chief constables of English counties instructed their men not to patrol game preserves for fear that their constables would appear the personal servants of landowners (Jones, 1979). Individual policemen on their beats also employed discretion to avoid the bureaucratic rigmarole resulting from arrests. For ambitious constables, chalking up numerous arrests of petty criminals was not necessarily the best way to gain promotion.

Even where there was an identifiable victim, police actions were inextricably tied up with the nature of the prosecutorial system. Constables could assist in arrests and the recovery of stolen property. But the system of private prosecution that the new police inherited meant that bringing a charge and prosecuting it was primarily the business of the victims or prosecution associations in the eighteenth and early nineteenth centuries (Hay, 1989; Hay and Snyder, 1989). Although the police were more likely to define behaviour by the working class as violent and law-breaking than similar behaviour by other social classes, they were highly unlikely to pursue common assault cases in which the alleged victim appeared either unlikely or unwilling to undertake a prosecution. A police warning was therefore an option, though in some cases police would use alternative charges such as obstruction, drunkenness, breach of the peace, and assault on the police (Davis, 1989a). Victims sometimes merely threatened prosecution to evict or control difficult house-mates, or to exact revenge often for quite unrelated wrongs. 'In a number of cases the prosecutors stopped short of actually press-ing a theft charge through to its conclusion, perhaps feeling that the arrest of an offender and possibly a night spent in the police cells might be enough to achieve their original aim in invoking the law' (Davis, 1989a, p.415). Private action was inhibited by a number of factors – the cost, the complexity of legal procedures, the duration of trial and anxiety involved. The police gradually took over the prosecution territory and, until the creation of the Crown Prosecution Service in the 1980s, assumed the unique responsibility for initiating and conducting prosecutions.

At the neighbourhood or street level, however, increased police powers had to be balanced against the need to negotiate 'a complex, shifting, largely unspoken "contract"' (Ignatieff, 1979, p.445). Indeed, a failure in this area sometimes led to widespread criticism or else to unnecessary local hostility, both of which made their job more difficult. Assaults on the Metro-politan police were prevalent enough – there were 2858 arrests for such assaults in 1869 alone (Smith, 1985, p.540). According to Weinberger (1981), despite the gradual acceptance of the new police by the 1850s, working-class hostility to the police never totally disappeared, as evidenced in the numbers of assaults on the police. Some of these assaults – for instance, in Birmingham for some years in the 1870s – were reportedly quite large affairs involving hundreds or even thousands of riotous people. 'Attacks were frequently carried out by gangs of youths who terrorised certain neighbourhoods, and who pelted and stoned police on sight, usually after closing time on Saturday night' (Weinberger, 1981, p.69). Hostility was, at least in part, related to the police role in enforcing harsher vagrancy statutes and licensing laws in the 1870s. Constables who fell foul of the villagers because of 'clumsy attempts to regulate Sunday drink-ing habits' had to be transferred from the local neighbourhood (Emsley, 1983, p.157). Against this background of a potentially violent street life, discretion enabled the police to strike an operational balance between the demands of the law, their superiors, and moral reformers on the one hand and the often different attitudes of the people in the local areas they policed on the other. 'They actively defined the activities they would turn a blind eye to, and those which they would suppress, harass or control' (Ignatieff, 1979, p.445). The alternative strategy, observing the full letter of the law, would only generate mass arrests, which would overstretch limited police resources and threaten the bureaucratic system of processing criminals.

Much police discipline – short of arrest and prosecution – was exercised on the streets. There were published stories about the 'Tyranny of the New Police' in London, assaulting and insulting individuals and confiscating children's toys, marbles and hoops (Emsley, 1983). To the extent that the labour market in early industrialization consigned young people to the casual, unskilled, unorganized end of the spectrum, and the unemployed to the front line of street confrontation with the law, policing the 'residuum' of the working class increasingly took on a more youthful hue. Throughout the history of youth policing in the late nineteenth and early twentieth centuries, the police took action against a wide range of street pastimes or misdemeanours – for instance, street gambling in the form of pitch and toss, loitering youths, the bicycling 'scorchers', 'young boys throwing stones or spitting from the London bridges on to boats and their passengers below' (Pearson, 1983). The following is an oral account of those on the receiving-end of policing in Manchester during the 1890s:

> We were always getting into trouble – playing football and kicking balls about, breaking a few windows, you know. Now, one time, if you stood at the corner of the street, you'd get locked up for it. They'd call it 'obstruction'. If you played football in the street, you got summoned for it, and if you went selling papers on a Sunday morning, you'd get locked up for it. Wasn't to sell papers, you see. Wasn't allowed to shout on the roads at night on account of people objected to it, you know...   (quoted in Humphries, 1981, p.147)

Other accounts (Cohen, 1979; Pearson, 1983; White, 1986) of policing in some working-class neighbourhoods related the lingering feud-like relationship between the police and young people in the inter-war years. In Liverpool, policing the lower-class city invariably meant controlling the street kids, moving them on, 'keeping one's beat clean' or 'taking them home for a belt' (Brogden, 1991). 'The police were to be avoided always, assisted never, inconvenienced where possible', as local residents recalled in White's (1986, p.115) account of life in 'the worst street in North London'. There was deep resentment of the arbitrary exercise of almost limitless powers of the police – 'the police had to make seven arrests a week, and it might as well be you as anyone else' (ibid., p.116). And when arrests were made, then all hell might break loose. In one case, the police constable was attacked by 'a hostile crowd of old women, girls and kids'. 'He lost his whistle, his tunic and his trousers were torn and he was bitten on the hand' (ibid., p.119). Children and young people just playing on street corners or acting as 'doggers-out' for gambling schools could always expect a 'tap' from a local policeman. Cohen (1979) suggests that 'cuffs and capes' seemed to have been the favourite methods of discipline by the Islington police in the 1920s, as they could be applied seemingly randomly against individual kids. 'The sense of shock registered is not at the actual violence meted out . . . [but] the sudden and arbitrary nature of its occurrence' (Cohen, 1979, p.123). But as Cohen (1979) also argues, the actual practices of social control at street level and the contexts of policing were contingent on a set of uneven changes – changes in the conditions and composition of the local working class, on the position of youth within the generational division of labour, and on the changing function of the police force in the developing structure of the capitalist state. Where police–youth relations did change from outright physical confrontation to tacit negotiation, antagonism remained unresolved: 'it was pursued by means other than street beatings and set-tos' (Cohen, 1979, p.123).

POLICE SERVICE WORK AND JUVENILE LIAISON

The antagonisms and dynamics of the relation between young people and the police were mediated by the enduring police 'service' role. The police had traditionally organized welfare assistance specifically for the poor – for instance, soup kitchens and summer excursions for poor children, and charitable funds to supply them with boots (Emsley, 1991). In the 1890s, the Liverpool Police introduced a system of clothing and licensing juvenile street pedlars (Brogden, 1982). Distraught parents might call in a local constable to deal with a difficult child. For many parents, however, the services that police provided could be a double-edged sword: following the 1870 Education Act, some police constables were required to act as School Attendance Officers, or 'truant catchers', to serve summonses on those parents whose children failed to attend school (Carlen et al., 1992). Where there were shortages of remand facilities, police stations and even private houses (particularly of married constables) were all pressed into service (Weinberger, 1995). A 'short and unpleasant form of detention' in the police cells was also regarded as a useful and economical means of disposing of some of the young offenders (Molony Committee, 1927, p.91). The police played an important role in the early juvenile court system – for instance, it was common practice for them to provide court reports about offenders' home surroundings and to implement court sentences of birching (Home Office, 1923; see also Bailey, 1987).

In the twentieth century, the development of police service work was closely linked to the wider process of bureaucratization, of which specialization was one of the key features of 'rational administration' (Brogden et al., 1988). Of course, the development of centralized specialist functional departments such as the detective section at Scotland Yard can be traced back to the early years of the new police. But the principle of specialization was increasingly adopted by the police in the postwar period in relation to juveniles, traffic, community relations, drugs and public order, sometimes on an ad hoc basis but more often achieving an institutional permanence.

Police remedies for juvenile delinquency were also inextricably linked with local traditions and circumstances. In line with the popular view from the 1920s that juvenile delinquency was a response to poor surroundings and inadequate character training, police involvement in recreational activities for working-class

children, and later Attendance Centres for juvenile offenders, had
always received a good press as the best means to counter delinquency. Norwich and Swansea developed police-run clubs as a
means of countering juvenile delinquency and the boys' sense of
antagonism towards the police. Other areas such as the Liverpool
Police developed what became known as juvenile liaison schemes
or units as the police spearhead in the realm of social welfare. The
juvenile liaison scheme, which began as an experiment in 1949,
was born out of the traditional police commitment to the social
containment of street residents and in reducing high rates of
juvenile delinquency. Since the Second World War, the police
had become increasingly concerned that children were running
wild, and that parental control was virtually non-existent in many
districts (Weinberger, 1995). Under the juvenile liaison scheme,
one full-time police officer was assigned to each of the seven
police divisions of the city to deal with minor first offenders
who admitted the offence, and whose parents agreed to cooperate
with the police over the help and advice offered. Prevention of
further offences was also to be achieved through liaison with head
teachers, ministers of religion and youth workers (ibid.). Over
time, the work of the juvenile liaison officers extended to children
who were below the minimum age of criminal responsibility and
other non-offenders. In these cases, the purpose of the juvenile
liaison scheme was 'pre-emption'. The police were seen as 'ideally
situated to learn of potential delinquents at an early stage and
take immediate action to prevent them developing criminal tendencies'.[8] Juveniles were warned by the liaison officers against
frequenting places which offered 'peculiar temptations' and
'causing nuisance in large city stores, streets leading to markets,
nut treating mills, and sugar refineries' (Liverpool City Police,
1962, p.11). In line with the emphasis on family casework at the
time, early juvenile liaison schemes were also geared to the policing or, in Foucault's (1977) term, 'normalisation of inadequate
families'. In 1952 alone, a total of 3767 visits were made to the
homes of juveniles under the Liverpool Scheme. The purpose was
'to foster in the mind of the child ideas which will lead to responsible citizenship and, where necessary, bring home to the parents
their individual responsibilities' (Liverpool City Police, 1962,

p.10).[9] The scheme was regarded as a resounding success by the police authorities, who published statistics showing the falling rate of juvenile recidivism during its first few years of operation.

Elsewhere, the reaction was mixed. In 1954, the juvenile liaison approach was considered by the Advisory Council on the Treatment of Offenders and details of the scheme were circulated by the Home Office to all chief constables for their information, who could then make up their own minds (Taylor, 1971). The Ingleby Committee Report (1960) cast doubt on the value of juvenile liaison schemes and argued that the role of the police officer was incompatible with that of a social worker.[10] The findings of subsequent research studies on the juvenile liaison schemes were equally mixed (Mack, 1963; Cain, 1968; Cain and Dearden, 1966; Rose and Hamilton, 1970). Whilst some magistrates and professional associations were critical of such policework, police forces with good experiences of such schemes denied that the work encroached on the rights and duties of the juvenile courts. By 1963, there were around twelve juvenile liaison schemes in England and Wales (Schaffer, 1980). Despite the new initiatives, there is evidence that arbitrary use of police disciplinary powers on the streets remained commonplace. The 1960 Royal Commission on the Police was in part triggered by allegations in parliament that a police constable had struck a boy in Thurso, and that this complaint had not been properly investigated by the Scottish Procurator Fiscal (Reiner, 1985; see also Judge, 1994, for the 'Thurso boy incident' and other similar cases). As Weinberger (1995, p.153) commented, 'the balance between the proper use of police discretion and their proper role as law enforcers remained uneasy, with no one prepared to condemn outright the preventive work of juvenile liaison officers, but no one prepared to insist that they become part of the set up in every force'.

JUVENILE DELINQUENCY AS CONTESTED TERRITORY

Historically, the juvenile court represented the junction point at which the penal and assistantial functions of state agencies came to bear on the child and family. To the extent that the juvenile court was regarded as the critical forum for meting out welfare treatment under the 1933 Children and Young Persons Act, there was an increased willingness to bring juvenile delinquents before court.[11] But it was 'help and reform' based on positivistic and medico-psychological notions of problem families and individual pathology. The main positivist impact on social work in Britain in the 1920s was to come through the development of psychiatric social work and the 'child guidance team' which originated in America. In particular, the highly influential works of the psychologist Cyril Burt (though now much questioned) emphasized the combined influence of environmental factors (especially defective family relations and defective discipline) and inner personal weakness on delinquent behaviour (Burt, 1925). This view of the delinquent as a unique human being with identifiable problems underpinned the demands throughout the inter-war period for pre-sentence investigation of the mental and physical condition of each delinquent, the home and social environment. Hence the need for special inquiries (mainly by probation officers), home visits, compulsory remand, and expert assessment of the child's medical, psychological and welfare needs. Then came the delivery of prescribed treatment to match the needs of each offender – almost exclusively in the form of the certified school or probation order, which, of course, only the court was able to prescribe. The importance of probation and residential treatment for some first-time offenders was stressed by the Children's Branch of the Home Office, lest the juvenile delinquent should turn into 'the hardened criminal of later years'.[12]

It is within this context that opposition to attempts at dealing with juveniles outside the juvenile court system has to be understood. The Report of the Departmental Committee on the Treatment of Young Offenders (the Molony Report) (1927), which proved to be a major stepping-stone to the Children and Young Persons Act of 1933, reflected the prevailing concerns and assumptions about the treatment of juvenile delinquents and the administration of the juvenile court system. Despite the general consensus within the Committee to extend the civil functions of the juvenile courts and the belief that, in so far as the courts were there to help, many more children ought to be brought before them than was the case, the Committee was reluctant to deal with young people outside the criminal jurisdiction. This was based on the consideration that the juvenile offender should have the opportunity to rebut the charges. Perhaps more importantly, there was concern that to dispense with court-like procedures could undermine the gravity of the offence and 'the feeling of respect for the law' in the eyes of the offender (ibid., p.19). In the end, the Committee was cautiously in favour of 'a form of preliminary action either by the police or by the education authority' in dealing with juvenile delinquency that went beyond a 'clip round the ear':

> ... in trifling cases, especially when it is a first offence, a police officer may properly prefer to turn a blind eye. Many police forces adopt a system of warning youngsters who appear to be getting into trouble. The warning is usually administered in the presence of the parents by the Chief Constable or a superior officer – a practice which seems to us to be a wise method of dealing with minor offences if applied with judgement and good sense.   (Molony Committee, 1927, p.22.)

But what the Molony Report did regard as 'outside the proper duties of the police' and 'usurping the functions of a tribunal' was the institutionalization of the warning system – not unlike the Superintendent's Court operated by the Glasgow City Police in the early 1900s – where 'a Conference is held in the Chief Constable's room at which the child and his parents, the police officer concerned in the inquiry and sometimes the probation officer or other social worker are directed to appear' (ibid.). Also, the Molony Report objected to the informal actions by the school authorities, whereby minor offences could be dealt with by the head teacher in the presence of the child and the parents, the attendance officer, probation officer, and the police officer. The Report 'strongly deprecate(d) any such proposal as creating a form of tribunal which could not be so satisfactory as a juvenile court' (ibid., p.22).

Against a background of the increasing use of police caution for a range of offences during the inter-war years (Smithies, 1982), fears that the police use of discretion was neither fair nor appropriate continued to be voiced. Magistrates objected to the message being sent out to the public involved in motoring offences: 'the vague idea entertained nowadays that first offences of all kinds go unpunished seems to be in danger of extension to the belief that they go unprosecuted.'[13] The suggestion in *The Times* that the police should exercise their discretion and 'turn a blind eye on certain forms of gambling' provoked bitter opposition from the legal profession (Williams, 1954). In cases where the offence was in dispute, magistrates warned against the police trying 'to assume powers properly belonging to the magistracy'.[14] Landlords who wanted to get rid of their tenants were reported to have abused the system by 'complaining on slender grounds or none, getting the tenant cautioned by the police, and then proceeding in the County Court for ejectment on the ground of the tenant being a nuisance'.[15] But it was towards the discretionary authority which the police had over young people that magistrates' criticism was mostly directed. The Second World War, along with the closing of schools and evacuation of children, brought significant disruption not only to home life for children but also to the smooth running of the juvenile court system. Although wartime conditions and shortage of probation officers made probation work increasingly difficult, more worrying for magistrates and probation officers was the development of alternative means of dealing with juvenile delinquents outside the formal court system. They were keen to:

> ... correct mistaken ideas which are gaining ground that delinquencies by evacuees should be dealt with by the school authorities, or by the police, without the cases being reported to the magistrates for trial, a procedure which cuts right across the Probation Act and the Children and Young Persons' Act and challenges the jurisdiction of the juvenile court.[16]

Magistrates were quick to condemn the practice in some police force areas of bringing children before an unofficial body styled the 'Juvenile Admonition Panel' as 'contrary to English justice'.[17] In Rochdale, for instance, the panel which 'met periodically' to decide on cases for police warning was brought into being through the director of education and involved the senior school attendance officer and the police. Once a decision was made, the child would be formally cautioned by the chief constable. The 'Juvenile Admonition Panel' was criticized by magistrates as 'an imitation of the juvenile court panel' and having 'no statutory status or authority'.[18] The chairman of the Manchester juvenile court panel argued that 'children were entitled to trial by an independent tribunal' and urged the 'parents [to] raise an objection to chief constables dealing with their children'.[19] The police practice of arranging for offenders to attend a child guidance clinic or generally intervening between the juvenile and the court was denounced as 'a retrograde move'.[20]

The argument that juveniles should not be denied justice was linked to the magistrates' fear that dispensing with court-based procedures could undermine the gravity of the offence:

> This system of police warnings is very open to misuse. It is a very dangerous practice for the police to assume the responsibility of deciding that a warning by themselves is sufficient. A juvenile court is provided with the proper machinery for dealing with offenders. For example, they can have a boy properly supervised by a probation officer, and this the police cannot do. I do not wish to exaggerate the importance of this question, but it is beyond dispute that grave mischief may result if a boy gets the impression that if he commits an offence he has nothing to fear than a warning from the police.[21]

But the juvenile court magistrates' objection to the use of police cautions was also tied up with a perceived threat to their own powers:

> We are jealous of our position; we are placed here as a juvenile court, representative of the juvenile court panel to try all children, and we must protect those children...It is

quite as much our duty to protect them as to punish them, and if someone else is taking it out of our hands, we have no power to protect those children at all.[22]

Similarly, the probation services were sceptical about the 'juvenile admonition panels' because their development was seen as part of a state reorganization to give the local education authorities the responsibility for delinquent youth. Although almost half of all juveniles charged with indictable offences were dealt with by probation during the war, the probation services were increasingly alarmed by public discussion of the transfer of all services concerned with children to the education authorities, including suggestions by the National Union of Teachers and of education directors that either probation officers should become employees of the education authority, or probation work should be done by school attendance officers (Bailey, 1987).

'CHILDREN IN TROUBLE'

There was renewed emphasis in the post-war years on unsatisfactory home conditions, absent fathers, family conflicts, lack of affection and parental interest, and the influence of changing moral standards as the main causes of a 'delinquent generation' of children born during wartime (Home Office, 1949; 1960; Philp and Timms, 1957). But the perennial construction of juvenile delinquency as a social problem requiring the intervention of different agencies is also linked with the working through of alternative state strategies for dealing with sets of problems thrown up by a particular historical moment. The Labour strategy for juvenile delinquency, the 1965 and 1968 White Papers, and the subsequent 1969 Children and Young Persons Act (CYPA), have to be understood within the context of social-democratic thinking on the relation between the state and the family (or, more particularly, inadequate and incompetent families). The overall political agenda in this period was based on the belief that the problems of material inequality had been largely resolved by a postwar settlement of full employment and rising standards of living. Social democratic debates centred on the role of the neutral state in improving and re-equipping the working-class 'residuum' who could not catch up with the fortunate majority or cope with the new technical apparatus of life. Although the task of delinquency discovery could be dispersed among existing bureau-professional regimes in education, employment, child guidance, care authority, health, housing and so on, the perceived need for family based intervention led to proposals for a 'family based social work service' as the major coordinating agency in place of the formal legal process. The aim of the 1965 White Paper, as Clarke (1979, p.92) has argued,

> ... is a more complex reorganisation of the balance between consensual and repressive processes – a new strategic balance which provides methods of operation more suitable to dealing with the problems of reproduction which are registered in delinquency. It is a commitment to a policy which suggests that intervention in the social and psychological processes which are held to underlie serious delinquency is best constructed without the oppressive weight and formality of legal process – that is, to create an internalised set of controls rather than externally imposed ones.

In the midst of severe criticisms from the magistrates, lawyers, police and probation officers, the concept of a 'family service' was dropped (Bottoms, 1974).[23] But the central idea of juvenile offending as a symptom of more general underlying disorders remained in the 1968 White Paper, *Children in Trouble* (Home Office, 1968) and, with few modifications, the 1969 CYPA. The juvenile court was to become an agency of last resort: for the under-fourteens, an offence was not to be a sign for intervention unless the conditions for care proceedings were also met. Criminal prosecution would be possible against the fourteen to seventeen-year-olds but only after mandatory discussions between the police and social service departments, and should be avoided for all except a small minority. In the form of disposal there was to be a shift from the penal to the assistantial, again with social work as the major coordinating agency. Care and supervision orders, intermediate treatment and family support were to replace borstals, attendance centres and detention centres; local authority institutional provisions were also to be reorganized within the framework of 'community homes'. In the event, because of the non-implementation of key sections of the 1969 CYPA by the new Conservative government, police cautions never received statutory recognition. Instead, it was left to the discretion of the local police to liaise with probation and social services departments and to create their own administrative process for deciding whether or not to prosecute.

WELFARE POLICING IN A LAW AND ORDER SOCIETY

The 1960s witnessed a sharp increase in the proportion of juvenile offenders being cautioned. The number of cautions given in 1968 for juvenile offenders was 33 703; one year later in 1969, the number given had risen by as much as a third to 44 998. In 1971, when the 1969 CYPA came into force, there was another large increase in cautioning to 70 957 (Ditchfield, 1976). The increase in the cautioning rate (i.e. those cautioned as a proportion of all those found guilty and cautioned) was sharpest among the youngest age group especially between 1967 and 1971 (see Figure 1.1). But the balance between the proper use of police discretion and their proper role as law enforcers remained an uneasy one. For the rank-and-file officers, the continued belief that juvenile delinquents were 'little devils' who needed punishment was at odds with the official purpose of the liaison schemes, which was to avoid taking the young people before the court (Weinberger, 1995).

The development of juvenile liaison was also mediated by gender divisions. In spite of the gradual and grudging acceptance of women in the police after the Second World War, female police were expected to maintain their gender role and deal primarily with girls and young women (Lock, 1979). There was evidence that policing female delinquents was oriented not only towards transgressions of the law but also problems of

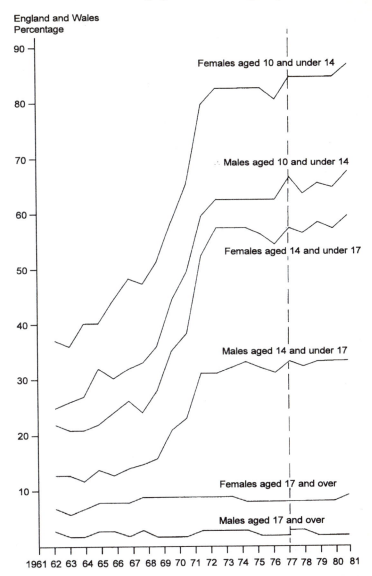

Figure 1.1   Offenders cautioned for indictable offences as a percentage of offenders found guilty or cautioned, 1961–1981.
Source: *Criminal Statistics England and Wales, 1981* (Home Office, 1982).

gender role maintenance. Taylor (1971), in his study of the West Ham Juvenile Liaison Scheme, found that 24 per cent of boys but 64 per cent of the girls being cautioned were non-offenders. These female non-offenders included those who stayed out late at night, refused to go out to work or help in the home, or were 'dirty' and 'unkempt' in appearance. Girls who were considered as in 'moral danger' varied, from those who were drunk to 'girls entertaining boys in the house in their parents' absence, or to a girl who was associating with a married man' (ibid., pp.5–6).

In the event, police supervision was regarded as extremely resource-intensive and supervisory work increasingly became the province of the social services. Some force areas still experimented with the so-called 'juvenile support schemes' in the late 1970s, involving, for instance, local beat constables in Hertfordshire or, in Cheshire, public volunteers as 'aunts' and 'uncles' to children who had been cautioned (HM Chief Inspector of Constabulary, 1978; 1979). But for other police forces, the priority began to shift. In Bristol and the Metropolitan Police, for instance, 'juvenile bureaux' were established to collect information about juvenile offenders from various agencies such as schools and social work departments and to recommend the action thought appropriate (Oliver, 1973; Ditchfield, 1976). In Devon and Cornwall under the then Chief Constable John Alderson, the police service role and the specialized function of the liaison units became increasingly synthesized within the framework of 'community policing'. Individual cautioning tasks were to be supplemented by multi-agency coordination and generalized proactive policing aimed not only at 'controlling the bad but also activating the good' (Alderson, 1980, p.38). In police–school liaison, what this meant was that instrumental functions of crime and accident prevention were often combined with direct attempts at mobilizing youthful consent to particular notions of a social order.[24] Police service functions were, and still are, vital to policing style in Britain. At an ideological level, service work restores 'the police institution to its natural location at the centre of social affairs', reinforces the 'symbiotic connection between the police institution and local community', and is vital to the construction and maintenance of the consent relation (Brogden, 1982).

Police service work, however, did not wholly displace other mechanisms for dealing with street offences and 'folk devils' – for example, mods and rockers, and later football hooligans and student protesters – who posed a threat to the authorities' sense of order (Cohen, 1973; Pearson, 1983; Muncie, 1984). In some areas, as Parker's Liverpool inner city study (1974) demonstrates, conflict and violence (or the threat of police violence) remained a taken-for-granted feature of routine police–youth interaction. The 1970s also saw an escalation in the number and seriousness of confrontations between the police and black youth (Hall et al., 1978; Keith, 1993). Significantly, the tendency to 'criminalize' every threat to a disciplined social order, the intensity of the conflicts to be policed in some inner city areas, and the willingness of the government to sanction 'tough' methods, were accompanied by the police acting as what Hall and others (1978) have termed the shock troops of the 'law and order society'. Thus, for particular sections of the population, the notion that their everyday experience of policing has anything meaningful to do with a consensual tradition which underlies police service work must be highly contentious.

2 Controlling Cautioning Practice and Police Discretion

The police caution is now the predominant means of dealing with young offenders outside the formal court system in England and Wales. In 1994, 95 500 young people under the age of eighteen were cautioned by the police for indictable offences compared to 40 300 found guilty in court. A formal caution can have serious implications: it is recorded by the police, and may be taken into account in subsequent police decision-making. It is citable in court and can be subject to judicial review (Evans, 1996). Despite this, the historical legacy of the police's claim of common law discretion in deciding when *not* to invoke the full processes of law means that the system of police cautioning has always operated on a non-statutory basis. Police cautioning has remained largely unaffected by the creation of the Crown Prosecution Service (CPS), as the CPS has no formal power to review or alter cautioning (i.e. non-prosecution) policy or practice. Instead, oversight of the cautioning system is the responsibility of the Home Office. The Home Office's initiatives have evolved around the setting of policy objectives, promoting national standards for cautioning practice and closer monitoring of caution decisions. In theory, this should lead to police decisions which are impartial, more consistent and open both to police managers and other agencies. The results in practice have been much more ambiguous because of the low visibility of police decisions on the street, the complexity of the police construction of 'cautionability', and the multi-purpose use of cautioning as a resource in policing.

POLICE CAUTION AND DIVERSION

As we saw in the previous chapter, Section 5(2) of the 1969 Children and Young Persons Act, which gave statutory recognition to police cautions, was never implemented. Nevertheless, this period saw a dramatic increase in the cautioning rates for young people. The Home Office, acknowledging the prevalence of local unofficial practices, recommended all forces to adopt a formal system of cautioning (Home Office, 1976). As Brogden (1982, p.141) argued, it was a case of 'state policy follow[ing] police legal entrepreneurship'. By the late 1970s, police cautioning had become so much a part of the official criminal justice system that previous formal cautions could, in many circumstances, be cited in court as part of an offender's offending history in the event that he or she re-offended (Home Office, 1978).

But the rhetorical power of cautioning in criminal justice discourse was (and still is) enshrined in its capacity to embrace several imperatives simultaneously. First, the expansion of cautioning is frequently associated with the development of 'diversion'. With the collapse of the rehabilitative ideal in the 1970s, the need for penal professionals to find new grounds of credibility was clear. The apparent ineffectiveness of the penal-welfare strategy to stem the rising tide of post-war delinquency was no longer seen as either a problem of resources (requiring increased funding and the expansion of child welfare services) or of implementation (requiring more research into the effectiveness of different treatment measures). In what Garland (1990) describes as 'the crisis of penal modernism', the limitations of prisons, borstals and traditional policing methods were exposed, not least by the Home Office's own criminological research. The crisis led to doubts about the efficacy of criminal justice institutions amongst many academics and practitioners; in others, a sense of despair that 'nothing works'. More damagingly, radical criminological critique located welfare professionals as part of the problem rather than as part of the solution. 'By default or design the reforming endeavours of the Fabians had been incorporated into a more pervasive and more punitive system of juvenile justice. Social welfare and social work had been annexed and put into the service of the law and order state' (Pitts, 1988, p.18). This was the period which witnessed an apparent 'net-widening' (Cohen, 1985) of penal control, as the elements of the new system created by the 1969 CYPA were absorbed into an expanded system that retained its traditional commitment to imprisonment as the ultimate sanction. In particular, social work was attacked for using the absence of proper legal controls to subject growing numbers of juveniles to excessive and premature intervention. Younger and 'pre-delinquent' children were processed into treatment-type programmes based on arbitrary assessments of 'needs', and those defined as 'difficult' and 'troublesome' were quickly passed on to secure institutions (Thorpe et al., 1980; Thorpe, 1983; May, 1971; Morris and McIsaac, 1978; Page and Clark, 1971; Tutt, 1978). 'Diversion', in the context of keeping young people away from court, care and custody, can thus be seen as social work's response to this predicament. Social work professionals redefined their mission in terms of 'leaving the kids alone'. In the process, social sciences arguments (especially from the labelling perspective) which suggest that the processes of arrest, trial and conviction can change the self image of juveniles, were 'rediscovered'.[1]

Second, and in a parallel debate, cautioning fitted in with the demands for a 'return to justice' (Geach and Szwed, 1983; Giller and Covington, 1983; Giller and Morris, 1981; Morris et al., 1980; Morris and Giller, 1983). From the viewpoint of the liberal justice lobby, the 1969 CYPA provided the focal point for their criticisms of the consequences of discretionary control of juveniles. The central arguments are that the safeguards of the formal justice process have been undermined by the rise of individualized treatment and social work's claims to specialized knowledge or expertise. The countervailing forces of legal rights have been lost in the massive expansion of discretionary powers and rehabilitative vagueness. Under the so-called 'justice' model, the way forward is to remove the disparity and indeterminacy in sentencing, the dangers of 'up-tariffing', and all the discretionary elements of control contained within the 'welfarist' youth justice system. The expectation is that, by re-establishing values of procedural justice, proportionality, visibility and predictability of legal administration, the extent of penal intervention would also be reduced:

By restricting the powers of the juvenile court and limiting intervention so that it is proportionate to the offences children commit, it is argued that a more rational disposition process will emerge and that justice for children will be provided.
(Giller and Covington, 1983, p.146)

'Just deserts' arguments have since been used to support the use of police cautioning as the proportionate response to minor forms of lawbreaking or to offences of certain kinds of persons of low culpability, such as the young, the old and the mentally ill (Ashworth, 1989). But there are problems with the mapping of the justice approach onto the development of police cautioning. The justice approach, with its exclusive focus on the offending, has been criticized for ignoring a number of politically incon-venient realities – i.e. 'those perspectives which address the personal, cultural, social, economic and racial factors which may increase the vulnerability of young people to involvement in crime or heightened surveillance by the police' (Pitts, 1992, p.138). Furthermore, critics have argued that back to *justice* can easily become translated into back to *punishment* (Hudson, 1987). Since the justice model, with its emphasis on due process formalism, is non-prescriptive of the overall tariff penalties and the purpose of punishment, there has been considerable 'over-lapping of would-be progressive and clearly reactionary argu-ments in favour of the return to justice' (Clarke, 1985, p.416). This is apparent in the debate about the dangers of cautioning in recent years. The production of 'conviction records' which are not subject to vigorous legal proof, the problems of lack of transparency and legal accountability in caution decision-making, have been highlighted by those writing from a critical socio-legal standpoint (Sanders, 1986, 1988; Evans, 1996). Concern has been raised that some suspects who are in fact innocent, may decide to 'admit' an offence and be cautioned for it rather than face protracted court proceedings. And since suspects and police officers are not always best equipped to judge guilt, the fear is that cautioning can lead to suspects' legal rights being reduced. However, similar arguments that innocent citizens may be pres-surized into accepting some form of conditional caution in lieu of a court appearance have been raised by right-wing critics, who complained about those multi-agency 'casinos of care' which 'crept up on the judicial system unawares'. For these critics, cautioning reduces the certainties of punishment and the 'justifiable public stigma' attached to a criminal conviction (Block, 1989; McKittrick and Eysenck, 1984). In this way, the emphasis on due process protection and legal order becomes conflated with a neo-conservative attack on juvenile delinquency as a threat to moral order:

> Many of those in favour of diversion are so inclined because they see the process as removing or minimizing 'stigma' from the offender... But have we really reached such a state in our progressive Western democracy when we should accept stigma-free theft, even if it is only shoplifting from Woolworths? We suggest not. Much of our criminal law, and a very substantial amount of common law, has as its basis in moral standards, and we suggest that even in our pluralist society today the vast majority of people in the country, no matter what their religious or ethnic background, would deem theft a crime and a moral wrong...
>
>   (McKittrick and Eysenck, 1984, p.393).

Third, cautioning fitted in with a 'bifurcated' or twin-track approach to crime management (Bottoms, 1977). The Conservative government's 1980 White Paper, *Young Offenders*, officially endorsed cautioning as a demonstrated method of keeping young people from becoming further enmeshed in the formal criminal justice process. The argument is that the court experience is a potentially negative and stigmatizing one, and that diversion from court by means of a caution reduces the likelihood of re-offending (Home Office, 1980a).[2] This may seem a somewhat surprising stance to be adopted by a political party which had launched a strong attack on delinquency in the run-up to the 1979 general election and, throughout the 1980s, condemned the 'soft' way that 'dangerous young thugs' were dealt with. On the surface, the diversionary notion of 'leaving kids alone' had no place in the Conservatives' policies of discipline and punishment. In effect, the punishment of young offenders has been much more ambiguous than the law and order rhetoric suggested. Youth justice policies dramatize or demonize a small number of 'hard core' offenders for whom longer and tougher punishment is deemed to be essential, and normalize 'the rest', for whom allowing them to grow out of crime is deemed to be more cost-effective. A control model based on a redefining and redistribution of the deviant populations has arguably allowed the government to get tough and soft simultaneously.

This political orientation towards a pragmatic bifurcation has been accompanied by wider developments of managerialism in criminal justice. Managerialism is less concerned with debating moral questions of individual responsibility or the purpose of punishment, than with streamlining the processes and rationalizing penal systems that already exist. It becomes important, then, to develop strategies of system intervention and information management to provide analyses and profiles of system functioning. Indeed, there has been a dramatic growth of technology to collate information on the internal performance of local police and youth justice systems (say, the time elapsed between arrests and court hearings; the number of officers on the beat), to coordinate and monitor administrative decision-making in order to bring about particular policy objectives and meet minimum standards in service delivery (e.g. the number of emergency calls processed). All these developments, as Feeley and Simon (1992) suggest, reflect profound changes in the nature and purposes of the penal system. Under this 'new penology', traditional and readily understood social goals (such as reducing crime rates, catching villains or rehabilitating inmates) are becoming of less significance to the penal system than the internal goals of formal rationality. In an era of lowered expectations about the effectiveness of state agencies in controlling crime, the aim of the penal system 'is not to eliminate crime but to make it tolerable through systemic coordination' (ibid., p.455). Their arguments do provide an alternative perspective on diversion in youth justice reform. Since the 1980s, a number of high-profile research and consultancy projects have been undertaken at Lancaster University and by private companies such as Social Information Systems, which aimed at rationalizing the operation of local care systems, measuring their outputs, and changing the behaviour of key decision-makers (rather than the juveniles) at various stages of the criminal justice process (Centre of Youth, Crime and Community, 1984; Tutt and Giller, 1984; Tutt and Giller, 1987). Under this 'systems management' approach, local police and social agencies would act as gatekeepers to monitor the number of direct entrants into the court system, regularly review the overall system performance, and set 'cautioning targets' (in percentage figures) for their local areas (Richardson, 1989).

Fourth, the expansion of cautioning can be seen as part of a wider strategy of the criminal justice system to adapt to high crime rates and high case loads. Garland (1996) argues that the overall objective of this strategy of 'defining deviance down' – including the development of fixed penalties and summary hearings for more serious offences, more selective use of police investigative resources – 'is to let minor offences and offenders fall below the threshold of official notice – to allow them to slip a "net" that is in danger of bursting at the seams'. In this context, police cautioning ensures that more valuable and expensive crime control resources need not be 'wasted' at the minimal end of the penal system. Indeed, the support that the Children and Young Persons Review Group in Northern Ireland (1979) gave to pre-court diversion was influenced as much by the perceived labelling effects of prosecution as by economic considerations. The argument was that the sheer cost and delay of formal processing is disproportionate to the seriousness of crimes that young people commit, and 'as most children who offend admit guilt, it is often an unnecessary waste of resources to proceed to prosecution and a finding of guilt' (ibid., para.6.3). By weeding out the 'Mickey Mouse' cases which are jamming the court system, efficiency savings can be made throughout the criminal justice system (see also Home Office, 1984; Audit Commission, 1993). Given the fiscal crisis in public sector expenditure in the 1990s, a truncated criminal justice system that bypasses the lengthy and costly processes of full investigation and trial – which, on average, takes four months between arrest and sentence, and costs £2500 for each juvenile (Audit Commission, 1996) – clearly represents the tailored pathway to managing the problem of crime.

THE POLICY OF CAUTIONING

The problem, then, is translating this strategy of managing the crime problem into consistent policing practices without trespassing on the sensitive matter of operational independence. The most important instrument of government policy is the circular: a total of three cautioning circulars have been issued by the Home Office to police forces since the 1980s. A Joint Working Party was set up between the Home Office and the Association of Chief Police Officers (ACPO), resulting in a consultative document in 1984 and subsequently the 1985 cautioning circular. Taken together, the Home Office cautioning circulars and the accompanying National Standards for Cautioning represent the settled policy of cautioning: to prosecute juveniles 'only as a last resort'; to encourage inter-agency liaison; to develop greater consistency in decision-making about cautions. Similarly, the Code for the CPS which was set up as a second 'filter' to the prosecution process in England and Wales, makes clear that the Service's objective should be to divert juveniles from court wherever possible. 'Prosecution should always be regarded as a severe step' (Crown Prosecution Service, 1986, 1990).[3] With these policy intentions in mind, three formal criteria must be satisfied before a caution is issued:

— there must be evidence of the offender's guilt sufficient to give a realistic prospect of conviction – in other words, cautioning must not be used as a substitute for a weak prosecution case or to warn off those who might commit offences in future;
— the offender must admit the offence;
— the offender (or, in the case of a juvenile, his/her parents, guardian or 'appropriate adult') must understand the sig-

nificance of a caution and give informed consent to being
cautioned.   (Home Office, 1985, 1990c, 1994a).[4]

In 1990 the Home Office went further to promote cautioning to
other age groups. The Circular 59/90 firmly asserted that: 'The
courts should be used as a last resort, particularly for juveniles
and young adults.' Senior police officers in Somerset and several
Metropolitan Police divisions responded by creating new caution consideration charts or multi-agency diversionary initiatives
to boost their cautioning rates for young adults and in inner city
areas (Westwood, 1991a, 1991b; Evans, 1993a, 1993b). Elsewhere, enthusiasm was tempered by doubts. There were com-
plaints from magistrates that many 'hard core' delinquents were
getting away with crime, 'laughing at authority and thumbing
their noses to the court'.[5] Given that many of the Conservative
government's ideas on diversion seem to have been borrowed
from progressive centre-left criminal justice pressure groups, it is
not surprising that organizations such as NACRO, rather than
rank-and-file police officers, have entered into an enthusiastic
alliance to establish and extend the government policy. Opinion
on the value of cautioning became increasingly polarized. On the
one hand, Home Office statistics suggest that the majority of
those cautioned do not re-offend.[6] On the other hand, there is
anecdotal evidence that the police are no longer making arrests,
because of disillusionment with 'revolving door' cautioning policies. A series of Police Federation journal articles and editorials
also denounced local cautioning policies as the 'Thug's Charter'
and urging a radical rethink of the role of cautioning in the
'police armoury against crime'.[7]

In Merseyside, an experienced sergeant claimed it was not
unusual for an offender in the custody suite to tell her to get
a move on because he had still two cautions to go before he
could be charged... Little Jimmy's future may be the proper
concern of police, but should that future take precedence over
the grief of a single mother whose home Jimmy has burgled,
or the distress of the parents of the child whom he has beaten
up? How can police satisfactorily explain to such people that

they are taking no action (for all practical purposes, that is what a caution amounts to) against a juvenile who is known to have committed other offences?

(*Police Review*, 20 August 1993, p.4)

The Conservative government was publicly and politically identified with (and blamed for) the 'crisis' within the cautioning system, leading to the constant political necessity to intervene in order to reaffirm policy directions. As part of the then Home Secretary's 27-point package of law and order measures announced at the 1993 Conservative Party Conference, a more restrictive approach to cautioning was promoted. The use of second or subsequent police cautions, though never extensive according to available research evidence (Evans and Ferguson, 1991; Evans and Wilkinson, 1988), was discouraged in the 1994 cautioning circular to underline the government's commitment to getting 'tough on crime'. Some critics argued that even the principle of restraint in dealing with young offenders has now been de-emphasized in the 1994 revised *Code for Crown Prosecutors*.[8] The message from the Home Secretary was clear: 'From now on your first chance is your last chance. Criminals should know that they will be punished. Giving cautions to serious offenders, or to the same person time and again, sends the wrong message to criminals and the public.'[9]

VARIATIONS IN CAUTIONING PRACTICE

One of the criticisms of police cautioning from researchers throughout the 1980s was that the discrepancies in rates between police forces were indicative of an inequitable 'justice by geography' (Richardson, 1989). The fear was that offenders committing similar offences with similar histories of offending might be treated differently according to local policies in operation.[10] With the increased emphasis on better management and monitoring, police decisions should, in theory, be more consistent and transparent to senior police managers and other agencies because they are being made on clearly articulated, nationally agreed principles. In reality, variations in cautioning policy and practice both between and within police force areas have remained. For males under the age of 18, the cautioning rate by police force area for indictable offences in 1994 ranged from 44 per cent (Durham) to 85 per cent (Surrey). For females under the age of 18, the range of cautioning rate was smaller – from 72 per cent (South Wales) to 93 per cent (Warwickshire) (Home Office, 1995c) (see Table 2.1). Local variations are even more pronounced when summary offences are considered, which after all represent the bulk of policework. So what accounts for such variations, and what do they tell us about the way the police exercise their powers?

Table 2.1 Persons cautioned for indictable (excluding motoring) offences as a percentage of those found guilty/cautioned by police force area and sex, 1994 (Home Office, 1995c).

Police force area	Males (aged 10 to 17)	Females (aged 10 to 17)
Avon and Somerset	69	88
Bedfordshire	72	89
Cambridgeshire	72	82
Cheshire	71	84
Cleveland	59	83
Cumbria	57	75
Derbyshire	65	82
Devon and Cornwall	74	88
Dorset	68	84
Durham	44	75
Essex	76	92
Gloucestershire	73	83
Greater Manchester	62	85
Hampshire	77	90
Hertfordshire	74	91
Humberside	69	88
Kent	71	92
Lancashire	66	84
Leicestershire	70	89
Lincolnshire	57	78
Merseyside	55	84
Metropolitan Police District	65	84

Table 2.1 Cont'd

Police force area	Males (aged 10 to 17)	Females (aged 10 to 17)
Norfolk	74	91
Northamptonshire	69	79
Northumbria	65	85
North Yorkshire	72	83
Nottinghamshire	60	85
South Yorkshire	66	86
Staffordshire	63	83
Suffolk	79	89
Surrey	85	91
Sussex	78	89
Thames Valley	59	80
Warwickshire	74	93
West Mercia	68	87
West Midlands	65	86
West Yorkshire	58	84
Wiltshire	78	89
Dyfed-Powys	70	79
Gwent	62	84
North Wales	66	78
South Wales	46	72

Since the discovery by early research that the police routinely exercise a discretion in the way they enforce the law, a central concern has been with the question of whether discretion really meant discrimination, in particular against the young, the working class and black people. The issue, however, is complex and difficult to resolve. Despite the evidence of a pattern of social differentiation in the use of police powers, Reiner (1985) argued that differentiation does not necessarily indicate discrimination and could result from legally relevant factors.[11] There is evidence to suggest that local variations in cautioning rates may be due to the proportion of first offenders in, or the types of offences committed by, the local juvenile population (Landau, 1981, 1983; Mott, 1983; Laycock and Tarling, 1984; Evans, 1993). The national survey on cautioning conducted in the 1980s, however, suggests that variations in cautioning rates *within* police force areas and between age groups relate more to differences in policy and practice than differences in crime pattern (Evans and Wilkinson, 1988; see also Laycock and Tarling, 1984). Between 1989 and 1990, the largest increase in the cautioning rate for juvenile male offenders (up by 20 per cent) was in Hampshire, which had the lowest cautioning rate in 1989, 'because of a switch from informal to formal cautioning' (Home Office, 1992, p.97).

Traditionally, children are more likely to receive a formal caution than the older age groups, and girls more likely than boys (see Figure 2.1). Seventeen-year-olds were four times less likely to receive a caution than sixteen-year-olds (Home Office, 1990c), although the incorporation of seventeen-year-olds into the jurisdiction of the youth court has resulted in a narrowing of the fall-off in cautioning rates at seventeen. Mott (1983) and Evans (1991, 1993) argued that one important factor contributing to differences between the use of cautions for juvenile and young adult first offenders was the differential rates of admissions and denials. According to police records in two Metropolitan subdivisions, Evans (1993) found that nearly 95 per cent of juvenile first offenders admitted the charge compared to 39 per cent of young adults. But what appears to be a legal precondition for the cautioning process can also be the arbitrary result of the police 'push-in' tendency:

> When [young adult first offenders] deny the offence the majority (60.6 percent) are dealt with by means of no further action because there is insufficient evidence. This begs the question of why they were arrested in the first place. It also raises questions about the readiness with which juveniles admit and whether they do so even when the case against them is weak.   (Evans, 1993, p.574)

Landau's (1981) early study of the Metropolitan Police's decisions to charge juveniles immediately or refer them to the juvenile bureau (in which case a caution was a possible outcome) suggested older juveniles were more likely to be directly charged than younger, and Afro-Caribbean juveniles were more likely to be directly charged than their white counterparts.[12] In a subsequent study, Landau and Nathan (1983) found that both legal

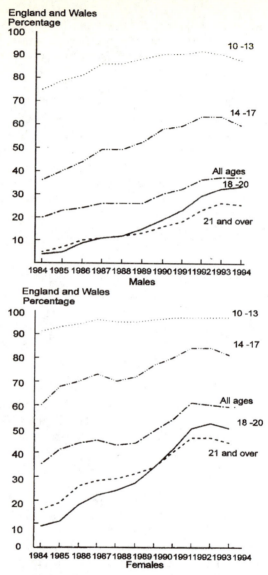

Figure 2.1 Offenders cautioned for indictable offences as a percentage of offenders found guilty or cautioned, by age and sex, 1994 (Home Office, 1995c).

variables (past record and type of offence) and non-legal variables (age, area, ethnic background and parental control) affected the police and juvenile bureau's decisions. In particular, they concluded that the chances of Afro-Caribbean juveniles being cautioned were considerably lower than white juveniles, especially when charged with a serious offence (e.g. crimes of violence and 'public disorder') and where they were assessed as having a 'problematic' family background:

> It is quite possible that black juveniles, more frequently than white, deny the offences of which they are accused. This denial may be due to more mistaken arrests of blacks for certain offences, to greater antagonism of blacks towards the police, or to a combination of both. (Landau and Nathan, 1983, p.144)

The relevance of the ethnic origin of the offender in cautioning decisions has been disputed by Fisher and Mawby (1982) who, when controlling for age, found that cautioning was not dependent on ethnic origin. This, however, may be due to a failure to control for social class, as Walker (1987) has pointed out in relation to research on race and policing.[13] Farrington and Bennett (1981) found some evidence that middle-class juveniles were more likely than working-class juveniles to be cautioned for serious offences, and that the level of cooperation shown by the juveniles and their parents was also significant. If the offender acknowledged his/her culpability or the parents' attitudes suggested that they would be willing to exercise control, then a caution, rather than a prosecution, was the more likely outcome. Similar conclusions were reached by Bennett (1979) and Fisher and Mawby (1982).

Where offences are comparable, Elliott (1988, p.85) found that significantly more females than males were cautioned, with the exception of offences of violence against the person, where females 'not only lose the advantage of leniency which they are given in other offence categories, but are treated more harshly than males in this category'. Other studies, however, found that the juvenile's sex did not have a significant effect on police decisions (Landau, 1981; Fisher and Mawby, 1982; Landau and Nathan, 1983). Such contradictory findings highlight the difficulties in conducting research on female offenders. One of the problems is the inevitably small numbers of girls and young women involved – 13.2 per cent of Landau's sample (Landau, 1981) and one-sixth of Fisher and Mawby's sample (1982) – which make complex statistical analysis difficult. Perhaps another way to understand caution decision-making in relation to females is to examine the interaction between legal variables and the underlying gender assumptions, such as the greater societal expectation of the female gender role to conform to authority by pleading guilty. That conventional gender stereotypes are generally held by those who operate the criminal justice system has been well documented (Alder, 1984; Edwards, 1984; Allen, 1987; Morris, 1987; Worrall, 1990; Kennedy, 1992). With the expansion of police cautioning schemes, the potential impact of gender stereotypes on decision-making at pre-court stage becomes even less subjected to public or legal scrutiny. Based on her observational study, Loraine Gelsthorpe (1989a) argued that although girls were more likely to receive a caution in cases where they had committed the same offence as boys, it was never simply because the offender was female:

> Cautions, especially, were perceived to be effective when applied to girls because they revealed an emotional response to the caution which signalled that the message about offending had been received.   (ibid., p.110)

Against a background of the organizational constraints and the police concern with achieving an impact upon the juvenile during the brief cautioning session, it may be that girls are more able to satisfy the expectations of police officers on the effectiveness of a caution, and their 'pathological potential' benefits female offenders in this way (Gelsthorpe, 1989a).[14]

DISCUSSION

That these studies have been unable to reach conclusive findings is perhaps not surprising. Discrepancies in cautioning rates between police force areas may relate to a combination of factors, and claims of bias are difficult to verify. Conversely, uniformity of rates between police areas in itself may not demonstrate police impartiality. Furthermore, the process of police construction of 'cautionability' is necessarily a complex one. Selection of 'facts', and their organization in the crime file by arresting officers are a result of subjective judgements based on social information about suspects – who they hang around with, whether they come from 'good' or 'bad' homes, what type of offences they are likely to commit, and where they are likely to do this. What this means is that any effective control of police cautioning must start with an examination of the processes of social background representations, the exigencies of street-level policing practice and assumptions underlying the assessment of *deserving* and *undeserving* cases.

NET-WIDENING

Another operational malfunction that research studies have identified is the problem that cautioning can have an inflationary rather than diversionary effect. Whilst diversion can mean keeping juveniles *out of* formal intervention, it can also mean diverting juveniles *to* alternative programmes. In the United States, the emphasis on early identification and treatment in many of the diversionary programmes had brought in clients not yet caught up in the justice system (Klein, 1979; Sarri, 1983; Lemert, 1981). This has led Austin and Krisberg (1981, p.71) to argue that 'diversion programmes have been transformed into a means for extending the net, making it stronger, creating new nets' of social control. The concern was that many projects served a *supplementary* rather than an *alternative* role, and that they offered too narrow or too little constructive service to the young people.

In the British context, some critics have argued that the diversionary elements of early Intermediate Treatment schemes (IT) were absorbed into a much expanded system of juvenile control (Pitts, 1988; Thorpe et al., 1980). As originally conceived,

IT was to replace detention centres and attendance centres and to provide a form of community-based treatment for young serious offenders. But given that key parts of the 1969 CYPA were never implemented, IT practitioners had to work with clients who were available. As a result, much IT activity in the 1970s was undertaken for preventive reasons or directed at juvenile offenders low on the tariff, including those cautioned by the police (Adams et al., 1981; Paley and Thorpe, 1974; Thorpe, 1973, Cooper, 1970).[15] Even with the intensification of many IT projects in the mid-1980s in an effort to shore up their credibility as 'alternatives' to custody with sentencers, IT provisions remained highly diverse (Bottoms et al., 1990).

In the case of pre-court diversion, one of the most discussed paradoxes in the 1970s is that more, not fewer, juveniles were labelled as delinquents (Pratt, 1986). 'Net-widening' arguably occurs because formal cautions have replaced informal or 'on the spot' warnings given by beat officers (Ditchfield, 1976; Steer, 1970; Farrington and Bennett, 1981; Parker et al., 1981). Such claims are difficult to verify because, as with the monitoring of other organizationally invisible behaviour of officers on the street, there can be no statistical test of the extent to which informal warnings have been replaced by officially recorded cautions.[16] Net-widening can also happen in another sense: the possibility that involvement in a diversion programme will be for longer and will be more intrusive than the order which the juvenile would have received if referred to the court. Again, the evidence for this is inconclusive (Allen, 1991a). In England and Wales, there is no equivalent to the 'conditional waiver of prosecution' used in some other European jurisdictions, whereby prosecution is withheld *provided that* some formal condition is fulfilled (HEUNI, 1986). However, it is technically possible for an offender to agree to additional action of some kind when receiving a caution, and such additions to cautions are commonly known as *Caution Plus*.[17] In principle, offenders (adult or juvenile) who are cautioned cannot be required to complete specific tasks (Home Office, 1990c). In practice, it is possible that a process of 'leaning on' can take place at the cautioning stage. The success of or failure to complete a Caution Plus programme may have significant implications for the 'deferred' cautioning decision (Marshall, 1984).

So what does Caution Plus involve? A NACRO survey (1993a) of 110 of the existing 117 social services departments found that some form of 'post-cautioning support' was available throughout 62 local authorities, and 13 others could offer some support in part of their areas. The nature of services varied enormously from confidential counselling to young people and/or their parents, the provision of information leaflets, to organized activities for cautioned young people. The idea of a caution supported by supervision by the police or other social agencies is nothing new. The general assumption is that the effectiveness of a caution is likely to be enhanced if it is backed by arrangements for referring offenders who have particular difficulties related to the offence to other welfare agencies. But Caution Plus can also involve attaching penalties to cautions, i.e. 'substantial activity' through which persistent and serious offenders can make amends for their offending. Here the police's emphasis is not so much on voluntary help as on just deserts and punishment, and any extension of Caution Plus schemes may be regarded as unsuitable 'without the threat of a sanction for those who do not comply' (ACPO, 1989, para.9.6). Seen in this light, the attempt to develop Caution Plus as a 'credible' alternative to prosecution can lead to intensification of its 'plus' element – or giving cautions some 'teeth' (Evans and Wilkinson, 1988).

A Case Study: the Milton Keynes Shop Theft Initiative

In practice, Caution Plus schemes can involve a mixture of practical help, moral sanction, shaming and shock tactics by the police, social welfare agencies and business organizations. One example is the Shop Theft Initiative operated by the Thames Valley Police in Milton Keynes, in one of the biggest central shopping centres in Europe. Although the local survey shows an average amount of most offences – including theft and burglary – compared against the national crime statistics (Shapland et al., 1995), shop theft was seen as a major problem by the retailers, who in turn lobbied for a more effective policing strategy against retail crime in the city.

The Shop Theft Initiative, described by the police as a 'realistic approach' to the problem of shoplifting, began in May 1994. 'It brings together the police, retailers, youth workers, prison officers and other agencies in an effort to get to the root cause of why individuals have stolen from shops' (*Police Review*, 12 August 1994, p.17). Between June 1994 and 1995, just under 400 people were dealt with under the Shop Theft Initiative with the majority (73 per cent) being juveniles (Thames Valley Police, 1995). The Shop Theft Initiative starts in a security suite situated in the shopping centre, where suspects brought to the attention of uniformed patrol officers by store detectives are taken to be photographed and fingerprinted. If the offence is admitted, details of identity and address are taken and checked with police records and the stolen property recorded and returned to the store. This procedure generally takes an hour, and the suspect is then bailed to attend the police station, normally in two weeks' time. However, 'if the individual is beyond re-education, a persistent thief known to us or uses violence during arrest, or is part of an organised gang, then he or she will be taken back to the police station and processed in the usual way under the PACE' (interview with Police Inspector). When offenders answered bail, they were then interviewed by officers from the Community Liaison Department to decide on the appropriate intervention:

> 'We'll explain to the juveniles and parents that a cautioning decision has been made. If the youngsters want to be put on our caution plus scheme, then we'll do an assessment and try to find out why they committed the offence. If they're not interested in what we have to offer, we'll administer the formal caution and that's the end of it.'
>
> (Interview with Police Inspector)

There are four main elements to the Caution Plus scheme in Milton Keynes. Taken together, they reflect the enduring influence of quasi-sociological and psychological theories of delinquency and the preventive role of the police in countering criminal careers. The first element is the 'youth and community services input' where young people were referred to the social services, Benefits Office, youth workers, Victim Support, Young Befriender Scheme or any other organization for counselling, help and support. In practice, boredom and lack of hobbies were often seen as the predominant causes of shoplifting, and young people were encouraged to attend a youth services session where they would be introduced to constructive leisure activities. The second element is the so-called 'protective behaviour input' by the police whereby officers helped the young people tackle problems of peer group pressure, bullying and behavioural difficulties. Apart from practical help and psychoanalytical counselling, the Caution Plus also involved 'tutorial from the prison officers', either in the form of a two-hour discussion with groups of young people or one-to-one sessions. In general, the prison officers' tutorial was reserved for the 'hard core' juveniles:

'The prison officers talk about life in prison, the weapons and drugs which are smuggled into the prison, the diseases prisoners get contracted, and so on. It's shock tactics, and for a minority of the youngsters they need it. Too often young people get a glorified account of prison life, so we need to blow away the myths about going to prison.'
(Interview with Police Inspector, Milton Keynes)

Just as their predecessors had sought to redeem the child pickpockets and vagrants in the previous decades, the police relied on a mixture of practical help and shock tactics arguably to 'nip serious criminal behaviour in the bud':

'If you look at the criminal records of a lot of the major criminals like armed robbers and burglars, they all started off with shoplifting. So if we can stop shoplifting now, we'll be taking out future car crime thieves and armed robbers.'
(Interview with Police Inspector, Milton Keynes)

The fourth element to the Caution Plus scheme is an 'offender meets victim' session where offenders were made to apologize to one of eight store managers attending the Caution Plus, on a rota basis, on behalf of all the shopping centre's retailers. Store managers were also there 'to explain the economic effects and consequences of the theft to the offender' (Thames Valley Police, 1995, p.3). As the Police Chief Superintendent who devised the Caution Plus scheme explained,

> [When] the criminal justice system fails to confront offenders with their behaviour they have to be made aware that shop-lifting is not a victimless crime. When retailers lose money, prices go up which in turn can lead to the loss of jobs – which relatives and friends of offenders could be losing.
>
> (*Police Review*, 12 August 1994, p.18)[18]

CAUTION AS A POLICE RESOURCE

To the extent that current debates about cautioning are framed within the context of diversion, the issue is: does it constitute 'true' diversion? Or does it lead to 'net-widening'? But such a focus ignores the important fact that, like many other police decisions, cautions and administrative decisions to take 'no further action' are often a multi-purpose *resource* for the police in their daily routines. Sanders and Young (1994), for instance, have noted that police decisions about public order arrest are often based on the perceived need to take immediate authorit-ative action in situations where voluntary submission is not forthcoming or when their authority is jeopardized. Where arrest is used as a means of 'getting on top of the situation', persons arrested and even detained at the police station are frequently disposed of without charge through the use of 'no further action' (NFA). At the everyday level of policing, where the emphasis is placed on investigating crime only *after* the arrest, it is perhaps not surprising that many suspects are released without charge due to lack of evidence. Seen in this light, NFAs are a product of purely speculative arrests – for instance, where the police 'trawled' local people with relevant previous convictions in order to eliminate them from a major enquiry; where suspects were arrested so that they could be held pending their questioning as witnesses; where all inhabitants of, and visitors to, a building were indiscriminately arrested in a drugs raid (Leng, 1992). Conversely, informal action may be taken in cases precisely to facilitate crime investigation – for instance, where the police did find (or could have found) evidence but decided to do a deal with suspects or potential informants (Dorn, 1994). Arrests may also be made as a result of pressure from the public and, according to Sanders (1994, p.795), 'if the police arrested reluctantly the outcome was often NFA'. The policing of drug user-dealers is a prime example. Amidst public concerns about open drug dealing and demands for safer streets, many police forces have mounted high-profile anti-drug operations to tackle the open, visible drug trade. It is here on the street, and amongst the small-scale entrepreneurs of the drug business and their customers whose social nuisance value may be highest, that massive police presence, intensive patrolling, moving on practices, targeting and surveillance, and buy-bust operations have tended to concentrate (Lee, 1996). To the extent that such focused street-sweeping generates a large number of what Collison (1995, p.205) has termed 'shit bum' arrests, police caution becomes an efficient administrative means of processing the 'little people' in the drug business.

Similarly, warnings and other forms of police 'ticking off' arising from police–public interactions may have little to do with the official policy to divert offenders from court. Rather, as we have seen in Chapter 1, informal, unrecorded police discipline has traditionally been part of the street justice meted out by front-line officers to what Lee (1981) has termed 'police property'. In the contemporary context, many young people clearly still experience street warnings as part and parcel of overpolicing, i.e. being stopped, hassled or picked on for 'minor' things ('jist standin aboot, like bein in a crowd sort of thing') (Anderson et al., 1994, p.141). In the case of public order policing, instead of reducing the level of hostility in police–public contacts, the use of police warnings may have the opposite effect of reinforcing the 'do as I say' style of policing (Jefferson, 1990).

DISCUSSION

Under the managerialist approach, inconsistent caution dec-ision-making, 'unintended' consequences and disparity in formal cautioning rates are to be tackled within a framework of clearly defined force tasks, the routinization of decision-making, and through organizational devices such as delegating the work of cautioning to specialist officers who are removed from the immediacy of the custody suite (Tutt and Giller, 1983). Such developments are not unique to policing. Qualities like discre-tion, individualized decision-making and personal relationships between welfare professionals and the young people which had been central to the treatment model, were under attack from the 1970s. In all aspects of the management of crime and deviance (including probation and parole), some form of risk prediction and classification techniques are now adopted to rationalize decision-making and to attain greater predictive efficiency in knowing where to target control effects. The same is happening in police cautioning. One notable example of the routinization of caution decision-making, commonly referred to as case dis-posal decision-making, is the elaborate Gravity Factor System devised by the Association of Chief Police Officers (ACPO). The main aim is to promote within all police force areas 'an objective and consistent means of reaching decisions on cautions' (ACPO, 1995, p.4). Although the technique itself is nothing new, the ACPO Gravity Factor System has positioned itself as a critical front-line steering mechanism for resource allocation in a crim-inal justice system that is increasingly locked into inflexible, 'one strike and you're out' rhetoric. The System provides a means of determining the depth, quality, rapidity, and site of controls, and targeting case management activities by assessing the cir-cumstances surrounding the offence (e.g. is it a local concern?) and the offender's behaviour (is he/she likely to re-offend?). The ACPO Gravity Factor System involves rating offences based on their 'seriousness' on a scale of 1 (low gravity, where a warning is the appropriate action) to 5 (high gravity, where the action will always be prosecution). A list of 15 aggravating factors (e.g. evidence of premeditation, 'grounds for believing the offence is likely to be repeated or continued', an offence is a prevalent local problem) and 13 mitigating factors (e.g. sign of regret or offer of reparation, provocation from victim) is given which apply to all offences. These factors may then lead to the upgrading or downgrading of the gravity score by one category. A further list of recommended gravity scores and aggravating and mitigating factors is then provided for specific offence categories, including assault, sexual offences, public order offences, offences under the Football Offences Act 1991, drugs, drunk and disorderly behaviour, theft, and burglary.

It is not difficult to see why the Gravity Factor System seems perfectly suited to the kinds of political demands facing the police in the 1990s. The style and texture of a matrix solution help address concerns about uniformity (a staggering 97 per cent consistency of decision-making in one police force was quoted in the ACPO document). It runs on discrete information which allows compliance with demands to make explicit the basis of police decision-making. It promises to yield results independent of the individuals who make the decisions, thereby eliminating doubts about racial, sexual or class biases of police officers. It appears to disclose the full set of assumptions and objectives that are applied to information, permitting real review of a decision's rationality. In practice, however, devices such as gravity scores, decision matrices and the like, lend the aura of objectivity, standardization and scientific sophistication to the process of decision-making without taking away much discretionary power from the arresting and custody officers. There is evidence to suggest that caution consideration charts are being used by the police *not* as an aid to decision-making, but as a retrospective justification for decisions based on subjective assessment of the young person or his/her family (Evans, 1993a). Ultimately, arm's length decision-makers can only review the police case that is presented to them.

3 Managing Youth Crime through Multi-Agency Partnerships

In the past decade, the multi-agency approach has increasingly come to dominate policy debates on crime control and criminal justice. In the diverse fields of crime prevention (Home Office, 1990d, 1991b), drugs control (HM Government, 1994; ACMD, 1994; London Drug Policy Forum, 1994), local policing (Home Office, 1993), prison disturbances (Woolf, 1991) and punishment in the community (Home Office, 1990e; Smith et al., 1993), 'partnerships' between statutory agencies, voluntary bodies, local businesses and communities are formed, linking organizations and groups with different goals, cultures and traditions. The emphasis on multi-agency intervention in the prevention and control of juvenile delinquency is, quite clearly, not a revolutionary breakthrough in the ways in which those problems had previously been discussed. This chapter looks at the reworking of the multi-agency approach as a feature of the discourse of criminal justice, and contrasts this with the local organization of juvenile delinquency as a contested site of intervention for different agencies.

REDEFINING OWNERSHIP OF THE CRIME PROBLEM

As we saw in Chapter 1, the construction of juvenile delinquency as a multi-faceted problem is nothing new. But the concept of multi-agency intervention was reworked to become a central organizing element in the Conservatives' managerialist solution to the penal crisis. After nearly two decades of increase in public expenditure within the criminal justice system, the Conservatives' rhetoric and policies on discipline and punishment failed to reduce the level of crime or improve public safety.

Notifiable offences recorded by the police more than doubled during the 1980s. Despite the fact that crime has an uneven social distribution, successive British crime surveys have shown that public fear of crime is now widely experienced as a prominent fact of modern life. In relation to youth crime in particular, it has been estimated that young people under the age of eighteen commit about seven million offences a year. Despite tougher sentences – epitomized by the 'boot camp' regimes – and an overhauled youth justice system at a cost of £1bn a year, the present arrangements have been denounced for failing the offenders and victims alike (Audit Commission, 1996). As some commentators have observed, this apparent failure of the Conservatives to deliver law and order has made the redefining of the *ownership* of the crime problem a political necessity:

> Diffusing political responsibility out from the formal apparatuses of the legal system to the community by supporting informal and voluntarist efforts and by encouraging citizens to accept personal responsibility for their own protection served, on this view, to deflect attention from the failures of government and to minimize damage to its credibility.
>
> (Lacey and Zedner, 1995, p. 305)

As a consequence, the message for the 1990s is that the public (as victims, local businesses, or members of Neighbourhood Watch and so on) will have to share in the responsibility in reducing opportunistic crime rates, to learn to avoid dangerous situations, or to meet their moral obligations as parents and 'responsible citizens'.

The voluntary efforts of the community and the individual are to be complemented by a multi-agency approach to crime management. But unlike multi-agency intervention in the 1960s which was anchored in aspirations to correct delinquents and decrease the likelihood of deviant behaviour, this 'new' multi-agency *partnership* approach is oriented towards concerns of systems management and indicators of internal system performance (cf. Moxon, 1985; Locke, 1990; Garland, 1996). With lowered expectations for any set of policies to dramatically reduce the level of crime, multi-agency action is no longer to be judged solely by recidivism but with reference to managing cases, developing and updating action plans, improving internal efficiency and minimizing unwarranted duplication of efforts. Since the late 1980s when a series of high-level conferences entitled 'Inter-Agency Linking in the Criminal Justice System' were sponsored by the Home Office, multi-agency work has been promoted through financial incentives at both national and local levels, to the extent that allocation of funds in some cases is only available through a commitment to joint work. One notable example is the Intermediate Treatment initiative (usually referred to as 'LAC 83' after the 1983 Local Authority Circular stipulating the provision of £15m as 'pump-priming' money), which stipulated cooperation between the statutory and voluntary sectors as an essential element in obtaining funding for the provision of community supervision for young offenders (Nellis, 1989).

The concept of multi-agency work also overlaps with the police ideological crusade to redefine the role of the police in the fight against crime. The apparent rising crime rates and falling detection rates, when combined with evidence of 'poor performance and failures that range from incivility and aggressiveness to corruption' (ACPO, 1990), raise fundamental questions about the cost-effectiveness of the traditional methods of policing. In principle, community consultative arrangements, together with a professional multi-agency approach to crime management, would produce a more receptive climate for the police to 'do their job' properly. This is seen as particularly important because of the crisis of legitimacy in the aftermath of the urban riots in the 1980s. For senior police figures such as Sir Kenneth Newman (former Commissioner of the Metropolitan Police) and John Alderson (former Chief Constable of Devon and Cornwall), multi-agency or 'community' policing strategy was the key to re-establishing the authority and legitimacy of the police on the streets:

It is not sufficient to think only in terms of crime control. We need to lift the problems to a higher level of generality, encompassed by the expression 'social control', in a benign sense, in order to provide a unifying concept within which the activities of the police and other agencies can be co-ordinated (quoted in Rose, 1992, p.36).

Scraton (1985) has described multi-agency work involving the police as a 'police-led' strategy designed to 'take over' other agencies and use them for their own ends of 'total policing'. In what Sampson and others (1988) have described as a 'conspiratorial model' of agency practice, the emergence of the multi-agency approach represents part of a general process of ever-increasing coercion by the state. There is some evidence of the mobilization of non-police resources towards police-defined goals, as when police surveillance, street clearance and targeting operations and other drug enforcement efforts become enmeshed with local councils' actions in the management of cities and people (Lee, 1996). But given the multiple points of resistance, the multi-agency policing strategy is far from total. First, as Holdaway (1986) and Blagg and Smith (1989, p.37) have noted, the multi-agency approach may be treated with 'suspicion or derision by lower-level workers, for whom it involves co-operation with people generally believed to be hostile and untrustworthy outsiders'. Junior police officers do not always regard liaison work as 'real' police work, and those officers from specialist units may be seen being 'punished' for 'incompetence elsewhere' (Philips and Cochrane, 1988).

Second, the multi-agency approach is perceived by some statutory agencies as part of the government's 'mixed economy' approach to criminal justice. It has aroused anxieties within the probation service about privatization and 'de-skilling', as some of its traditional roles are handed over – or 'contracted out' – to voluntary or private organizations whilst probation officers concentrate on the management of 'heavy-end' offenders in the community (Smith et al., 1993; Lee, 1995). Related to this is the question of 'hiving off' certain 'non-core' police functions and the government's interest in 'an increasing interface' between the public and private sector in policing (Lee, 1995b). Given the government's determination to curb public expenditure, many officers and the Police Federation now regard the increased involvement of the private sector (especially the private security industry) and 'active citizens' in crime control matters (such as the extensive use of the Special Constabulary in Derbyshire) simply as 'policing on the cheap' (*Times Magazine*, 23 March 1996, p.32). There is therefore a need to develop a 'more socially nuanced understanding' of multi-agency work, which takes into account the complexities of locally based initiatives, 'the power differentials running between state agencies', and the competing sectional interests that exist within the local state apparatus (Sampson et al., 1988, p.482).

THE ORGANIZATION OF MULTI-AGENCY COOPERATION: THE NATIONAL CONTEXT

The question remains what multi-agency cooperation in the pre-court forum actually entails. At the simplest level, the assertion of a practice as 'multi-agency based' implies a particular institutional framework. In their national survey of police cautioning policy and practice in the late 1980s, Evans and Wilkinson (1988) described two main institutional reference points for the multi-agency approach: through a 'bureau' whereby experts from different agencies are co-located in the same team, and through regular meetings between the police and representatives of social agencies variously referred to as juvenile liaison 'panels', consultation or offender review groups. Although both 'bureaux' and 'panels' are 'hybrid organizations', the key difference is that the juvenile 'bureaux' draw their full-time staff on secondment from a variety of agencies and may have broader monitoring and training functions (Evans and Ferguson, 1991). The most notable model for this approach were the Juvenile Liaison Bureaux (JLBs) in Northamptonshire in the 1980s (Thorpe, 1994). The JLBs, the first of which was set up in Wellingborough in 1981 and eventually implemented country-wide by the mid-1980s, included seconded staff from the local police, social services, probation, education and youth services (Bowden and Stevens, 1986). As Blagg et al. (1986, p.24) noted, the JLBs were the first examples of such inter-agency co-operation where the police agreed to be directly influenced in their decision-making by other professionals in all youth offences which came to police attention.

In contrast to the resource-intensive juvenile 'bureaux', juvenile 'panels' are arrangements where professionals meet to discuss cases referred by the police but do not work in the same team. As the NACRO survey (1993) of 110 social services departments suggests, the multi-agency 'panels' are by far the predominant form of local pre-trial consultative arrangement. In some areas, however, the organizational difference between multi-agency 'bureaux' and 'panels' may be more apparent than real (see below). To complicate matters further, multi-agency co-operative arrangements may change over time. In Northamptonshire, for instance, the early JLBs had 'a specific aim of trying to "normalize" the lives of children in difficulty'. Hence workers from the Bureaux were also responsible for supervising children, offering help to families and diverting children to local activities and IT projects (Northamptonshire County Council, 1983). By the late 1980s, the JLBs had arguably shifted to a policy of 'minimum intervention' into the lives of juvenile offenders (no further treatment, no service, no follow-up, wherever possible) and of avoiding intervention in areas of 'near-delinquency' such as truancy, disruptive behaviour at home and at school, and absconding. This attracted the criticism that 'non-intervention can become a euphemism for "benign neglect", for simply doing nothing' (Davis et al., 1989, p.231).[1] Given the increased pressures on the JLBs to deliver good results,[2] the JLBs were amalgamated with the Adult Reparation Bureau in 1993 to form the Diversion Unit oriented towards 'balancing the needs and rights of offenders against those of the victims and the community' (Wright, 1993, p.186).

THE LOCAL SETTING

We now turn to research carried out in four divisions – Red and Yellow Divisions, Grey Division, Blue Division – in three different police force areas. Research took place between 1990 and 1992 at a time when multi-agency work was given a significant impetus by central government policy documents. The Home Office Discussion Paper (Home Office, 1990e, p.9) recommended voluntary organizations and the private sector to be involved in the early stages of the criminal justice process – by providing referral mechanisms to enable young people who have been cautioned to receive advice, counselling etc.; helping parents of troublesome children to 'exercise their responsibilities more effectively', and providing relevant information to the Crown Prosecution Service in order to facilitate 'public interest' assessment. The Home Office Cautioning Circular 59/1990 made multi-agency consultation the central plank of its cautioning policy. It encouraged chief police officers to consult other agencies both at 'a policy level', in order to 'discuss broad cautioning strategy and objectives'; and 'in the making of cautioning decisions' in order to improve the 'quality' and 'consistency' of the decisions. The circular endorsed the extension of the diversionary policy across all age groups (Home Office, 1990c). The expectation by some commentators that the consultative arrangements used with juveniles would be extended to all age groups, particularly to young adult offenders, also led to a general mood of optimism at the time (Evans, 1991; NACRO, 1992).

In 1990, the average juvenile cautioning rates of the three police force areas included in the research study were remarkably similar: 85 per cent (including Red and Yellow Divisions), 86.5 per cent (including Grey Division) and 84 per cent (including Blue Division), compared to the national average of 82 per cent (Home Office, 1992). All four police force divisions reported policy reviews in relation to juvenile offenders following the issue of Circular 59/1990. However, changes in local cautioning policy and practice emanated as much from local exigencies (e.g. difficult relationship with the courts, pressures from senior police officers) as from the influence of the Circular itself. For example, the policy review initiated in the Grey Division just before the research started was triggered by concerns of senior officers at Police Headquarters, especially the new Chief

Constable, to exercise better control over local diversion/prosecution policies; to standardize the ad hoc multi-agency consultation arrangements and improve working relationships with social agencies, and to catch up in the national cautioning 'league' table.

Red Division

The police force had prided itself on its special police policy towards juveniles since the late 1910s: 'Sunday courts' were held at police headquarters, where offenders were reprimanded and encouraged to join a police-run Lads' Club rather than taken to court. The consequent drop in the local delinquency figures was taken to be a sign of success of policework with young people. In particular, the Lads' Club was held up to other police force areas for its positive effect in reducing juvenile crime up to the end of the Second World War.

The multi-agency based juvenile bureaux system was introduced in the police force area in 1981. In Red Division, as in the other three police divisions in the research study, senior managers of the police and social agencies sat on the panel/bureau arguably as a safeguard for objectivity and balanced decisions. So whilst frontline police officers were considered to be 'emotionally involved' in the cases and social workers who worked with children and families as 'too attached to their clients', managers saw themselves as 'one step removed from the person actually preparing the files or doing the report' (interview with Police Chairman, Red Division). The Juvenile Justice Bureau (henceforth JJB) in busy, city-based Red Division comprised a police Juvenile Liaison Officer (a female police constable), a police chairman (Chief Inspector of the Prosecutions Department), one senior probation officer, one team leader from the education welfare service, and three team leaders from the social services area teams, who met regularly to discuss individual case disposals. In all cases involving juveniles (including criminal matters and 'at risk'), the arresting or reporting officer would first complete the paperwork and fill in the appropriate forms.[3] Cases apart from those directly charged by the custody officer[4] (just under 10 per cent in 1990) would be passed for processing by the Juvenile Liaison Officer, who would then check the juvenile index for previous referrals. A duty Inspector could then decide to give an instant caution or to take 'no further action' (about 30 per cent in 1990). In cases where the juvenile had a previous record of convictions and/or cautions, where the offence was considered 'serious', or where another case was pending, the file would be passed on to the Crime Support Unit or Criminal Investigation Department. Of these deferred cases, almost half resulted in a decision to caution. The remaining cases in which the police recommended prosecution would then be discussed in the JJB where reports were routinely prepared by the social agencies. There were no formal arrangements for 'Caution Plus', although social agencies could indicate in JJB discussions where help would be available for an individual after a caution had been administered.[5] At the time of research, meetings usually lasting for an hour and a half were held once a week in a conference room at the police station. The atmosphere of the meetings was businesslike and sometimes tense, partly because of the hectic schedule of cases but also because of the tension between the social services and probation service over resource allocation.

Yellow Division

In contrast to Red Division, the Yellow Division in the same police force area covered an historic market town and half of the total area of the county classified as 'remote, mainly rural district' in the 1991 Census for England and Wales. The town currently has one of the most extensive closed circuit television schemes in the country: cameras were installed in the town centre and on housing estates in 1992 to monitor a range of activities – for example, unlicensed taxi cabs, vandalism and youths congregating on the estates, a local drugs problem and littering. The local police generally saw the Yellow Division as the home for 'problem tenants' and 'problem families', and therefore as a problem for the social services. Similarly, the three juvenile court magistrates interviewed in the research study referred to a sharp increase in broken families over the past ten years: a 'vicious circle' whereby 'inadequate parents would produce inadequate children'.

The Juvenile Liaison Bureau (JLB), described by the Police Chairman as 'a strong and humane bureau', was the first to be piloted in the county. It comprised a police chairman (Chief Inspector of the Prosecutions Department), one divisional manager of the education welfare service, one team leader from the social services and one senior probation officer, who met regularly to discuss individual case disposals. At the time of research, JLB discussions were held once a week in a meeting room at the probation service. The procedures of decision-making were similar to those of the Red Division, except that the Juvenile Liaison Officer (a female police constable) who conducted the initial juvenile index search and case processing, did not generally attend the JLB meetings. In 1990 a total of 560 juvenile offence cases were dealt with by the Yellow Division police. In cases where the police would not or could not pursue any further, a duty Inspector would decide to give an instant caution or to take 'no further action' (just under 40 per cent of all juvenile offence cases in 1990). Immediate charges were directed against 2 per cent of the cases outside the JLB by the duty custody officer. Otherwise, the file would be passed on to the Crime Support Unit or Criminal Investigation Department. Of these deferred cases, about 50 per cent resulted in a decision to caution. The remaining cases would then be discussed in the JLB where reports were sometimes prepared by the social agencies.[6] There were no formal arrangements for 'Caution Plus', although social agencies could indicate in JLB discussions where help would be available for an individual after a caution had been administered.

Grey Division

The area covered by Grey Division was seen as a by-product of urban redevelopment and the new town concept designed to cope with the overspill of London. The local police officers typically described themselves as 'busy but not doing anything exciting'. The general perception was that even though the level of petty crime (e.g. car theft, graffiti type of offences, criminal damage) seemed to have gone up, 'nothing major ever happens, perhaps one major fight or murder once a year!' As the police Juvenile Liaison Officer put it, 'the mass media must be bored with us!'

Local policework with juvenile delinquents can be traced back to the Juvenile Support Scheme piloted in Grey Division in 1978, under which police officers visited juvenile offenders who had been cautioned and introduced them to leisure pursuits. By the late 1980s, Juvenile Support Officers no longer carried out direct supervision but were responsible for the routine administration of multi-agency liaison, the processing of all juvenile cases (criminal and at-risk) and for keeping a juvenile index. Multi-agency liaison arrangements in the police force area were varied. They ranged from multi-agency panels which considered all juvenile offending cases to informal meetings between the Police Juvenile Support Officer and the Intermediate Treatment social worker where police recommendations for prosecution were discussed. At the time of research, the overall stated aims of the Force Diversion Strategy were to prevent juveniles from offending; to divert offenders from court whenever possible (including multiple cautioning); to avoid the imposition of penalties and welfare interventions which might aggravate the problem; to respond to delinquent behaviour in ways that would enable young people to become responsible adults; to promote and support everyday organizations in their understanding of and reaction to juvenile offenders. Caution-Plus schemes, piloted on an experimental basis and administered by the social services in some parts of the police force area, varied from:

> three one-hour sessions on a Saturday morning to a realistic approach which fitted the individual and the circumstances, such as an arson offender who was invited to the local fire station and shown a video which brought home the circumstances of such an act, and in another case of criminal damage where the offender repaired the damage under supervision, to another case of theft where he agreed to wash cars for payment in order to pay back the victim.
>
> (Police internal memorandum, February 1990)

In Grey Division the Juvenile Liaison Panel comprised a police Juvenile Liaison Officer (female police constable), one senior social worker and one Intermediate Treatment project leader from the social services, two senior education welfare officers, and one senior youth and community worker. At the time of research, weekly Panel meetings were held in the senior social worker's office. Referrals brought before the Panel by the police Juvenile Liaison Officer generally covered cases that fell outside the police categories of 'instant caution' or 'immediate charge'. Panel recommendations, occasionally based on home visit reports provided by the social services, were then passed on to the Chief Inspector in the Divisional Prosecutions Department for approval.[7] Although there were no formal provisions for 'Caution-Plus' in Grey Division at the time of research, informal support after cautioning was offered by the social services in a minority of cases.

Blue Division

Traditionally a millinery town, the area covered by Blue Division police expanded considerably in the 1950s as a result of the local motor industry. The economic recession, however, was seen to have brought about the collapse of many small industries, resulting in a concentration of unemployment and poverty in the large areas of high-rise council housing estates. According to the sub-regional statistics (Central Statistical Office, 1990), a third of all local authority tenants and almost one-half of the unemployed in the county were from this town. The Blue Division had the highest proportion of young people among the four research localities: almost 22 per cent of its population were under 15 years of age. From the point of view of the social services such an age composition, plus the apparent decline of family and kinship ties and high proportion of single-parent families, had generated a high childcare workload for the local social services team. But from the police point of view, the high profile of young people presented a different set of problems: as one police officer put it, 'groups of disorderly or drunken young people are always congregating and rampaging in the town centre or fighting'. Many of the police officers interviewed in the research study suggested that Blue Division lacked community spirit, meaning that 'the local people are not very helpful with police enquiries'. Riots in the summer of 1981 during which police officers from neighbouring forces were brought in were also cited as evidence of the lack of community spirit. Unlike the other three research localities, Blue Division was, and still is, a distinctly multi-racial community. According to the 1991 Census, at least 15 per cent of its population were born in countries outside the United Kingdom. In the late 1980s Blue Division became a prime site for multi-agency crime prevention initiatives. Its Crime Reduction Programme set up in 1989 included police-led summer activities for young people, a Motor Vehicle Project for young offenders, youth crime prevention panels and a disruptive pupils programme in secondary schools, 'designing out crime' initiatives in local shopping centres, and a town centre ban on drinking in public places at one stage.

The Juvenile Liaison Panel, consisting of the police chairman (Inspector in the Community Involvement Unit), a principal education welfare officer, the manager of the local Community Juvenile Centre (representing both the social services and probation service), and occasionally the senior court liaison officer from the social services, was rejuvenated in late 1989 after some years of inaction. At the time of the research, meetings were held every fortnight in a conference room at the police station. Referrals brought before the Panel by the police Inspector generally covered cases that fell outside the police categories of 'instant caution' or 'immediate charge'. Panel recommendations, occasionally based on home visit reports provided by the Community Juvenile Centre, were then passed on to the Chief Inspector in the Divisional Prosecutions Department for approval.[8]

CONTROLLING COURT BUSINESS

At the time of research, the relationship between the Juvenile Liaison Panel and the juvenile court magistracy in Grey Division was at its lowest ebb. The juvenile court magistrates complained that the police cautioning schemes had reduced the workload of the local juvenile court to such an extent that the local juvenile court panel was forced to amalgamate with another juvenile panel in the county. Many juvenile courts in other areas experienced similar decline in court business and cancellation of sittings as a result of the increase in juvenile cautioning rates.[9] This has arguably provided the economic explanation for extending the new youth court jurisdiction to include seventeen-year-olds (Bell and Haines, 1991).[10] Although constantly referring to the 'interests' of the juveniles, their parents and 'Mr. Public', local juvenile court magistrates in Grey Division clearly perceived police cautioning and its multi-agency basis as a threat to their own authority and independence within the criminal justice system:

> 'It's clear that our authority is being undermined by a group of people. The structure of this group is rather amorphous, somewhat vague. I mean, who is in charge of the panel? Who actually runs it? And what qualifications do they have? What training do they have? I think most of us feel that part of our role is being eroded. Juvenile magistrates are carefully chosen professionals. We have years of experience, and we are trained.'
> (Juvenile court magistrate, Grey Division)

This concern about the expansion of cautioning schemes was a common theme in all interviews with the magistrates:

> 'The official bit of coming to court, their parents having to come to court, which is all very annoying and awkward, might stop them [offending]. It does no harm to bring them to court earlier rather than later. When youngsters are cautioned that many times, they'll come to court a year or two older than when they started offending and by then they are more sophisticated and confirmed criminals.'
> (Juvenile court magistrate, Blue Division)

> 'Most of us feel that cautioning is being used too much and too often for the same child. And this is bad for individual

youngsters, not because we want to get on to punish them, well we do have to in some cases, but in terms of the child's development, in terms of diverting youngsters from criminal behaviour, [cautioning] is probably not the best thing to do. The other thing is that this undermines our role, and we are professionals in our field. We feel that although we are amateurs in that we are not paid for the job, we have the experience and training. And these people are undermining our role.'   (Juvenile court magistrate, Red Division)

'All of us who have children know that you say, "If you do that again, you won't have your pocket money, or I won't take you to the circus, or whatever." And if they do it again, that has to be what happens. Cautioning a repeat offender simply makes a mockery of the entire justice system.'
(Juvenile court magistrate, Yellow Division)

This was how one senior probation officer made sense of the magistrates' resistance to cautioning in his area:

'Magistrates didn't like the cautioning system at first. They were anxious about it, they were frightened about it...because they thought their authority was being undermined. And we spent some time trying to explain it to them. In the early days, we had such a dramatic effect on the number of juveniles brought before the court, in terms of diminishing the number of juveniles brought before the court, that they became really concerned about their powers, that there wasn't really enough business for them to do on a regular weekly basis.'   (Senior Probation Officer, Yellow Division)

Within a national context, it is now very rare for juveniles under fourteen to appear in court. Hughes and others (1995) observed that in Northamptonshire the de-escalating approach of the JLBs had reduced the juvenile court population from 1395 in 1980 to 86 in 1991. The result has been profound scepticism towards cautioning among sections of the magistracy in Northamptonshire. In particular, Evans (1991, p.602) found that some magistrates 'feel frustrated because they have not been included in the group setting up the Juvenile Bureau or on the management committee and cannot exercise the amount of influence that they wish to'. Similarly, the *Report of a Thematic Inspection on Young Offenders and the Probation Service* (HM Inspectorate of Probation, 1994) found overwhelmingly that sentencers believed that the level of cautioning was excessive and were opposed to the number of repeat cautions, even though the statistics suggested otherwise.

The historical dimension to the magistrates' opposition to attempts at dealing with juveniles outside the court system has already been discussed in Chapter 1. The judicial opposition to cautioning was, and still is, linked with demands for the preservation of magistrates' discretionary powers and of more sentencing options and more severe penalties in place of a 'mere warning'. The Justices' Clerks Society (1980), at one stage, proposed that police cautioning should be abolished and replaced by a new power for the courts, after finding a case proved, to dismiss the juvenile with a warning or admonition which is not legally a finding of guilt. It is within this wider context of the magistrates' own sense of dwindling authority that their resistance to cautioning has to be understood. The juvenile court magistrates in this research study suggest that they are quite happy to 'go along' with the cautioning schemes if such schemes could really reduce the level of juvenile offending in the area. Given the fact that there will always be juveniles brought before the court (including those who deny the charge) and that juvenile delinquency is defined more by the magistrates' own subjective notion of the ever-deteriorating youth problem, it seems almost inevitable that cautioning is dismissed as a 'soft' approach to delinquency control. In particular, social workers are often singled out by the magistrates as adopting an 'unrealistic' or 'softly, softly' approach to juvenile offenders and their families. Some researchers argued that attacks on social workers may be mediated by specific bench–agency relationships and interactions with the social services departments (Brown, 1991, pp. 63–6), or by the magistrates' moral assessment of individual social workers (Parker et al., 1989, p.94–5). Without further information, one cannot be certain whether or how such perceptions affect the ways in which young people who are eventually brought to court are assessed and punished. According to national figures, the most frequently used sentencing disposal for offenders aged under fourteen was absolute or conditional discharge (which may involve less intervention than a Caution Plus). Even for those aged fourteen and under eighteen, over one-quarter of male offenders and about one-half of female juveniles were discharged for indictable offences in court (Home Office, 1995c). One possible interpretation of this sentencing pattern is that many minor offending cases (plus the not guilty pleas which the police have refused to 'NFA') are still being pushed into the court system. There may not be a simple correlation between the number of previous cautions and the severity of the court sentence. But as Roger Evans (1991, pp. 602–5) pointed out, there is a common belief amongst the magistrates that young adult offenders appearing in court are 'more serious', 'more violent' and are 'those that the system has failed to deter as juveniles', even though their criminal histories and nature of their offences may suggest otherwise.

DISCUSSION

Multi-agency consultation in the four police force divisions is primarily concerned with individual case review, not with the broad cautioning strategy and objectives as the official cautioning circulars envisaged. This narrow conception of consultation is not unique to the administrative processing of juvenile delinquents. As a community liaison officer put it succinctly in McLaughlin's (1994, p.79) study of police – community consultation in Manchester:

consultation is the idea of the police consulting the community or meeting with the community to discuss all aspects of policing so that we will be better informed about public feelings and ideas and as a result be better able to make decisions about policing the community . . . consultation is not about the community making decisions affecting policing, but it should lead to the police taking better decisions affecting the community.

The 1994 cautioning circular has reinforced this narrow conception of consultation by making clear where the power lies: 'the decision to caution is in *all* cases one for the police' (Home Office, 1994a, para. 3, emphasis in the original). This may come as a severe blow to the social agencies, since many youth justice workers believed that the increased use of cautioning can be directly attributed to the influence they exercised over the police in the context of multi-agency consultation (Blagg and Smith, 1989).

4 Constructing the Case for Caution

In principle, the shift to the multi-agency approach to criminal justice in recent years should have benefited the autonomy and professional standing of the expert cadre. Under what Pratt (1989, p.229) has termed 'a corporatist model' of youth justice, bureau-professionals and child care specialists enjoying increased discretion are the key players in a pre-court administrative apparatus as they 'confer the label of delinquency without recourse to the formalities and intricacies of the legal process'. However, as critics have argued (Pearson et al., 1992; Blagg and Smith, 1989; McConville et al., 1991), the outcome has been much more contradictory because the agendas of those agencies with a core law and order mandate have been prioritized at the expense of others. This chapter looks at multi-agency consultation in action through an examination of the organization of police caution decision-making. On what basis are caution decisions being made? What is the impact of prior police decision-making on multi-agency work? And ultimately, is there scope for the social agencies to challenge the conceptions and categorizations underlying policework with juvenile delinquents?

POWER RELATIONS IN MULTI-AGENCY CONSULTATION

In line with the general findings of other research studies (Crawford, 1994; Sampson et al., 1988; Blagg and Smith, 1989), this study confirms the primacy of power relations in multi-agency work. As we shall see in the next chapter, inter-agency struggles over the contested meaning of the delinquency problem, what to do about it and by whom, are shaped by power differentials and historically based hierarchies of knowledge. But power relations

75

in multi-agency work also manifest themselves in seemingly non-conflictual interactions, that is, in 'getting things done', arriving at a decision acceptable to all within the liaison forum.

Blagg and Smith (1989) suggested that many juvenile justice workers believed that their influence over the police in the context of multi-agency consultation had directly led to the desirable result of increased use of cautioning. Research studies, however, have found only limited evidence that consultation produces significantly different outcomes to those that would result from the police making decisions on their own. Evans (1992; 1993a; 1993b) documented an increase in young adult cautioning rates following the implementation of two diversion schemes in the Metropolitan Police: in Westminster Division (without a young adult diversion panel), the cautioning rate increased from 13.4 per cent to 20.7 per cent; in Bromley (with a new multi-agency panel), the cautioning rate increased from 27.6 per cent to 32.6 per cent. 'Whether the increase is a direct result of the schemes or the continuation of an already upward trend, is difficult to assess' (Evans, 1993a, p.495). The increases were also described as 'disappointedly small' given the expectations of the panel and the commitment of senior police officers.

In multi-agency consultation, decisions are not the responsibility of the police alone. In this sense, as Evans (1993a) has argued, consultation plays a role similar to that which could be played by the Crown Prosecution Service: it puts distance between the investigative and case disposal phases of the prosecution process. But the reliance of the Crown Prosecution Service on the police for information and the close alignment of their roles and operational philosophies within the adversarial system have been well documented (McConville et al., 1991; Gelsthorpe and Giller, 1990; Sanders, 1988). Similarly, the social agencies in this study regard their consultative role as inherently circumscribed:

'It's the police who carry the trump card. Clearly they ultimately have the decision whether to prosecute or to caution. It...I accept it, and I think   probably at the end of the day, it's...well...probably it couldn't be any other way because it's the police who are most...how should I put it...it shouldn't necessarily be that way...it's that way...and I suppose I accept that. But I do think the police should take...should listen very carefully to what bureau members have to say.'   (Social services team leader, Yellow Division)

'I think considering the way things are operating over the country as a whole, we would never be likely to change it from the police having the last say, at least theoretically.'
(Senior probation officer, Yellow Division)

'The police always do have the final say. Whether that means that person should be chairing the bureau I do not know. Maybe we ought to have an independent chair. At the end of the day we all have to live with the fact that we are only an advisory body to the police.'   (Senior probation officer, Red Division)

The dominance of the police in multi-agency consultation can be understood in two ways. First, significant decisions are already taken by the police before cases are referred for consultation. Not all types of cases are regarded as 'cautionable' by the police, which means that some cases are automatically screened out of the multi-agency consultative processes for immediate prosecution. Public order offences (including all offences committed on football grounds in Red Division), juveniles pleading not guilty, those with pending offences or who had been previously sentenced and therefore considered 'already in the system', are in the main dealt with outside the multi-agency forum. This 'sifting' function of the police is confirmed in other research studies (Evans, 1993a, 1993b; McConville et al., 1991), although the extent to which 'instant' caution and prosecution decisions are taken by the police alone varies from one police force area to another.

POLICE CASE CONSTRUCTION

Second, the case referred to the multi-agency forum is the *police* case. The 'construction' of a case means not just filtering potential information, but imposing order and meaning upon it. At the heart of the official version of the offence found in the crime file is the nature and extent of the specific charges laid against a juvenile. The exact wording of the charge may be crucial to the smooth functioning of the cautioning process, in that a juvenile or his/her parents may not accept a particular charge as accurate, may question its validity and as a result find their case pushed into the formal court system. In their research, Parker et al. (1981, p.103) found that juveniles and their parents may respond to the 'unnecessary severity of the charge by pleading not guilty'. Alternatively, as Sanders and Bridges (1990) have suggested, there may be juveniles who, rather than go into the prosecution process, accept a caution and thus an admission of guilt, even though not privately agreeing with the accuracy of the charge.

Information in the police case summary, such as previous criminal history, or the attitude of the juvenile or the parents during the police interview may be routinely produced by the police as 'facts', which in turn form the basis for multi-agency discussion. Consider, for instance, the following excerpt from a police report on a male juvenile charged with 'actual bodily harm' on school premises in Red Division. Notice how the report constructs a caricature of the incorrigibility of the juvenile and objectifies a career of escalating delinquency (from schooling difficulties to suspension to total expulsion) behind the present offence:

N is a boy who has schooling difficulties. His family moved to our area and he was suspended and later expelled in October 1990. He has been told not to come onto school premises, but as you can see he has totally ignored this. When interviewing N, I was told by his mother that the victim deserved all he had got. Her attitude is that it is alright for her son to have a go at other boys if they are bigger than him. My impression is that N needs to be taught a lesson. This may be too late already, as I feel in some respects he is set in his ways. Court and custodial sentence is probably the only course of action open to us. If these are not forthcoming then I can see problems in the very near future.

(Excerpt from police crime file, Red Division)

There is no legal limit on what the police might introduce as evidence of 'problems' or pre-delinquent tendencies. As Evans and Ferguson (1991) pointed out, arresting officers often have a very detailed knowledge of the social backgrounds and habits of juvenile suspects. 'They know where they live and who they hang around with. They know the schools they go to and whether they come from "good" or "bad" homes' (Evans, 1993b, p.576). This local knowledge, coupled with an overriding concern with delinquency control, is a crucial aspect of the case construction process with juveniles. The police hold a general assumption that lack of an official record does not necessarily mean the juvenile has not been involved in recurring delinquent behaviour. Cases dismissed in court or suspected criminal activities are routinely referred to in multi-agency discussions. In another example, G (male, aged 16) refused to accept the charges of 'going equipped with a buzz hammer' and stealing a motor vehicle. The arresting officer noted in the crime file that:

> Although this juvenile has no previous convictions, he is strongly suspected of being a member of a team of thieves who specialize in thefts from unattended motor vehicles. There is no doubt this juvenile is extremely active in the theft of property from motor vehicles. His associates are known and it is anticipated he will be arrested again in the near future for similar offences. He was uncooperative when asked about previous attempts at theft from motor vehicles. A caution in this instance would be a waste of time.

(Excerpt from police crime file, Blue Division)

Social agencies very rarely challenge the police version of 'what happened'; they do not have access to complete crime files and the statements. Even in cases where the agencies did question the seriousness of the offence – for instance, whether or not the juvenile was the chief instigator of the offence, the extent of the damage, how many other juveniles were involved – the discussions were invariably confined within the pre-established police procedures and the legal labels attached to offences. In the above example, the manager of the Community Juvenile Centre challenged the basis of the suspected criminal activities, but agreed that the juvenile should still go to court given his denial of the offences.

There is another aspect of the police case construction that merits mention here. A case assessed by the officer-in-charge to be appropriate for caution can be revised, moved up or down the 'pre-prosecution tariff', as other extraneous circumstances unfold. The following case, dealt with outside the JLB but noted in Bureau discussion, illustrates this. C (male, aged 15) found an abandoned pedal cycle frame and kept it instead of reporting it to the police. The victim, from the same village, recognized the frame and reported it to the police in Yellow Division. This was the conversation between the police officer and C noted in the interview record:

Police: 'Why didn't you report finding this frame to us?'
C: 'Because I didn't think it would be worth it, it was all scratched.'
Police: 'Didn't you think it was someone else's property?'
C: 'I thought someone had chucked it away.'
Police: 'So as far as you are concerned, it had been dumped?'
C: 'Yes, because it was scratched and all that.'
          (Excerpt from the police interview record, Yellow Division)

C was charged with theft of the pedal cycle frame, and a decision was made to caution him. On the day when C was supposed to turn up for his caution, his mother rang the inspector and complained that they would not accept the caution because C had not committed any offence. The inspector then suggested that he could bring an alternative charge of 'theft on finding', but later changed his mind – 'it's not worth it because we can't prove it really'. The case was eventually marked 'NFA' (no further action), but was kept on the juvenile index held by the local police. Examples such as this illustrate starkly that police decisions serve a multiplicity of purposes which may bear no relationship to the official purpose of diversion at all. And when offences which have been NFA'd for lack of evidence are reported to the panel or bureau, they are presented as if they were records of antecedents.

THE DOMINANCE OF POLICE VALUES

The dominance of police values as another obstacle to the capacity of social agencies to review the police case has been well documented (Evans and Ferguson, 1991; McConville et al., 1991). Indeed, the discussions of cases in this research study almost invariably refer to the police recommendations for the case. These in turn are guided not only by legal considerations, but also by a police concern to make the criminal justice system victim-centred as opposed to offender-centred:

'We have to demonstrate to the criminals that the society would not tolerate such behaviour; we have to be seen by the public as doing something.'

(Police chairman of JLB, Yellow Division)

'It's what the society expects. There would be public anger if we caution too many people.'

(Police chairman of JJB, Red Division)

'There's this sort of softly softly approach to young criminals these days that I think is wrong. I get fed up with people saying, "these kids have only nicked a Mars Bar", well, that's still theft to me and the small shopowners are still the victim. And what about the old pensioners whose houses are burgled in the middle of the night. They may never recover from the shock. I think in those cases, the youngsters should be made to apologize to the victims or something; otherwise, how can you say there's justice for the victims?' (Police chairman of JLP, Blue Division)

The police claim to make the criminal justice system more victim-oriented cannot be taken at face value, however, as some victims are taken more seriously than others. On a political level, the police have found space in the victims' movement to respond positively to particular categories of crime victims, to mobilize community support for the police in the fight against crime, while at the same time marginalizing radical anti-police community groups. In particular, the police have arguably formed an alliance with voluntary organizations such as the National Association of Victim Support Schemes (NAVSS) which could be used 'to reclaim problematic victims and be trusted to "speak for" the police against their critics' (McLaughlin, 1994, p.117). As a 'respectable' voluntary organization enjoying considerable official patronage from the police and the Home Office, the NAVSS worked with a narrow conception of what Christie (1986) calls the 'ideal victim' (the elderly are a prime example) rather than the 'disreputable' ones (e.g. victims of police malpractice). Loader (1996) argues that this distinction between 'legitimate' and 'disreputable' victims is also apparent in the police understanding of youth victimization. Historically, young people have been positioned outside the boundaries of the 'ideal victim'. In official and popular discourse about crime, young people hanging around in groups tend to be viewed as 'trouble' rather than as regular users of public space, vulnerable to its attendant risks. For the police, this dominant paradigm of young people as 'trouble' together with their regular contact with young people in circumstances of conflict leads to two results: 'first of all, in the dismissal of much teenage victimisation as "kid's stuff"...[and] secondly, to the view that young people's victimisation is in some way or other their own fault' (Loader, 1996, pp. 93–4). The police failure to take youth victimization seriously can have important implications for the credibility of other police service tasks, a point to which we shall return in Chapter 7.

On the level of individual case disposal, it is the police who speak for the victims. For although successive Home Office cautioning circulars have made reference to the Victims' Charter, the views of the victim are to be treated as one of the many factors being taken into account by the police. The ACPO's (1994) guidance document on cautioning went one step further by making clear that victims' opinion should not form part of the case disposal decision-making process on the grounds of 'fairness' and 'consistency in the police approach'. Victims' views for or against prosecution are never discussed in panel or bureau meetings. Victims' interest therefore seems to operate more as a retrospective justification for a police course of action than as an active basis for it. In this sense, victims' interest is no more defined by the victims than the child's need is defined by the child.

For lower ranking officers, the police concern with fighting crime and protecting the public also dovetails with a pragmatic concern with maintaining their authority on the streets. This was how a police sergeant explained the situational aspects of the problem:

'This lad was stopped for riding on the road with no documentation and no insurance. So I gave him a caution, and he did exactly the same thing the second time a few days later. How can I caution again? He'd be just laughing in my face! He's also causing a nuisance to the public, so it's not something minor. I cautioned the first time, saying this is absolutely the last time. Then the second time, I said, "Next time you'll go to court for sure." Where do I go from there?'

(Police sergeant, Grey Division)

Ultimately, arm's length decision-makers can only review the case and recommendation for case disposal that is presented to them by the arresting and custody officers. Social workers and probation officers can sometimes challenge the police recommendation by highlighting the triviality of the offending behaviour (for instance, by arguing that it is a status symbol for young people to carry a penknife) or 'scaling down' the seriousness of the previous criminal record (that receiving a caution for five different charges on one single occasion is not the same as receiving five cautions). But reviews and the 'scaling down' of the seriousness of an offence by social agencies still take place within a framework of the predominant police values and procedures. The following example in Red Division illustrates this.

N was charged with 'actual bodily harm' and needed 'to be taught a lesson', as the police case file put it. The offence, however, was perceived by the education welfare officer (EWO) as 'not over-the-top ABH'. This was the dialogue that followed:

EWO: 'Although there is sufficient head injury for an ABH, I think it's basically a school-boy squabble.'

Social services: 'Yes, my impression is that both boys were in the wrong. It might even be the case that the injured party approached (the offender) first. It's difficult to tell.'

Police chairman: 'Perhaps we could introduce an alternative charge of minor public order, so we don't have to prove who caused the injuries. Since he's not admitting the injuries, let's just say it's merely behaviour not that of an average citizen and we can give him a caution. How's that?' (Red Division)

THE LEAST INTRUSIVE INTERVENTION

Social agencies generally perceive their role in terms of making the least intrusive intervention in the lives of young people, and arguing for an outcome as far down the 'pre-prosecution tariff' (e.g. an informal warning for first offenders committing less serious offences, followed by a formal caution, then a supported caution) as possible. But all this has to be done by taking into account what they might already know or expect about the police views on the appropriate case disposal. The result is that the time will come when all the agencies know that prosecution is due. On these occasions mitigation is but a ritual rather than an extended plea, which might be seen as wasting the panel's time ('There's nothing we can say to get him off the hook!', as one youth worker put it). Managers of social agencies, with one eye on maintaining their credibility on the panel and the other on fighting the more 'deserving' cases, tend not to waste the panel's time with 'no-hopers'. In one case, the social agencies even questioned the whole point of bringing these 'failures' before the panel for discussion:

Juvenile Liaison Officer:	'M has got thirteen previous cautions for arson, theft and criminal damage. He has got a permanent smirk on his face. He's obviously not one of those kids to be easily reformed. This time he has smashed the windows of an old lady's house.'
Social services:	'He has got such a long list of previous. I've seen him in court, and he just sees it as a joke. A caution wouldn't have any effect on him.'
Senior EWO:	'Should this case really be brought before the panel? Judging by his long list of previous, it's obvious that there's no way he would be given a caution again.'
	(Grey Division)

The need to work round police views on what would be an appropriate case disposal is also translated into the way supported cautions are organized. At the time of research, none of the four police force divisions officially administered a Caution Plus or supported caution. Although juveniles charged with particular offences such as reckless driving or 'taking without consent' were sometimes encouraged to join a motor group, these activities were not officially recorded; they were not organized as conditions of a caution nor accorded a specific place within the pre-prosecution tariff. Various reasons were given why Caution Plus had not been discussed or developed in the four research areas: lack of resources, lack of commitment, perceived danger of 'net-widening' and, in Red Division, the tension between the probation and social services. This did not prevent less formal involvement by the social agencies. In one case, a female juvenile with three previous cautions was charged with stealing goods (mainly food items) worth £22 from a supermarket. The police chairman was clearly concerned with the fact that cautioning 'hasn't worked' in the past, and was therefore reluctant to give her another chance. After much discussion, this was the dialogue that followed between the police chairman and the social service team worker:

Police:	'My concern is that a caution must not be administered and simply forgotten about.'
Social services:	'We can offer a few sessions. Would that help?'
Police:	'I might be prepared to give a caution, provided that further visits are made by the social services.'
Social services:	'We call it a caution, but we'll be doing some more investigation. Perhaps the education welfare officer can also do some follow-up. We'll arrange for a written apology to the manager from the juvenile and the parents as well.'
Police:	'All right then, as long as I am reassured that something would be done about this girl.' (Red Division)

In most instances, the decision to do some form of follow-up work or to involve the education welfare services is more of a tactical move to 'reassure' the police and to boost a caution rather than as part of a well-planned, concerted effort to support the juvenile. No one on the panel asked questions about the nature of the proposed follow-up work, its potential impact on the family, or its relevance to the female juvenile. Instead, the follow-up work formed part of a tactical move to 'buy' a caution for the juvenile by offering 'an extra little something' to the police.

A MESSY CASE?

Bottoms and McClean (1976, p.6) conclude from their observations that adult court workloads are such that 'the smooth administration of justice essentially depends on the cooperation of the mass of defendants', i.e. the cooperation of pleading guilty. This notion of oiling the machinery of cautioning is also relevant to our discussion here. At the heart of the cautioning process is a distinction between those who will, and those who will not, cooperate with the cautioning authority. Here, the role of the social agencies in categorizing or re-categorizing juvenile delinquents and their families can be crucial. In this example in Grey Division, the panel was faced with a problem when a thirteen-year-old male was charged with stealing a pedal cycle. He admitted to taking the cycle from his neighbour and dismantling it, but claimed that he intended to return it the following day. Hence the police were confronted with an administrative difficulty, i.e. a technical denial of intent. To the extent that the evocation of the offence represents an occasion to test the educability of an individual, a denial of guilt can also place the juvenile in the category of 'undeserving' cases. In this particular case, the juvenile liaison officer felt the offence was trivial and not worth pursuing in court. The following dialogue then took place between her and other agencies:

Youth and community worker:	'Can't we do something about it? Nudge it perhaps?'
Social services team leader:	'Can't we NFA?'
Juvenile Liaison Officer:	'How can we NFA when there's sufficient evidence?'
Youth and community worker:	'Can we take him to the police station with his parents and tell him off without giving him a caution?'
Senior EWO:	'I'm sure I can have a word with the lad. We've got to meet the police requirements to get him a caution. We know this lad; we haven't had any problems with him

in school. I think I can
deliver what you want.'
(Grey Division)

At this point, the senior education welfare officer proposed to
'have a word with the lad and his parents', to 'explain to him
that the police cannot caution if he denies the offence'. Everyone
on the panel was happy that a court appearance could be
avoided. No one questioned whether it was against the spirit
of due process for the education welfare officer to approach the
juvenile and his family without disclosing his involvement in the
panel. Instead, questions of procedural justice became conflated
with technical questions of fitting the case into tidy prescriptions
of how to avoid a court appearance.

If we have witnessed an example of the social agencies suc-
cessfully keeping a juvenile from court, I would suggest it was
also a pragmatic interpretation of the administrative logic of the
criminal justice system to resolve an otherwise 'messy' case. It is
important to note that these negotiations essentially aid the
smooth flow of business for the panel, defined not only in
neutral terms of securing a speedy through-put of cases but
also in terms of producing guilt. After two visits by the education welfare officer, the juvenile admitted the offence as charged
and 'no further action' was taken; everyone on the panel was
happy with the result. The key issue here concerns the task of
social agencies in the processing of juvenile delinquents. In the
context of identifying and managing deviant bodies outside the
formal court system, the increasing dominance of instrumental
rationality in case disposal decision-making is inherently
unfriendly to the expert status of social work, probation and
education welfare services. Here, the position of the ACPO
(1995, p.6) is illustrative: 'Matters such as school record and
home background should not generally influence the case disposal decision'. Instead, standardized information such as gravity score is used to categorize the juvenile delinquents, assess
their risk status and distribute control efforts. The credibility of
social agencies in such a system, then, depends on their ability to
win over 'difficult' or 'uncooperative' clients, and to translate

their definitions of 'guilt' into administrative definitions of policy objectives.

MORE MESSY CASES...

Just as juveniles who challenge the police case pose a threat to the authority of the police, those who fail to attend a cautioning session are often described as 'a pain' and their parents seen as 'opting out of their responsibility'. On a practical level, juveniles who fail to turn up for a caution present administrative difficulties to the case disposal process: officers have to send another letter requesting their attendance or rearrange another date for the cautioning session. That is why juvenile liaison officers frequently appeal to the social agencies by emphasizing the 'heavy workload of the individual inspectors who administer the cautions'. The underlying assumption of this administrative logic is that the juvenile and their parents are to blame: 'there is no other alternative but to prosecute'. But there are problems with this construction of individual responsibility. In one example, a first time offender (male, aged 13) was charged with stealing a jar of beans but failed to turn up with his mother for a caution. The following is the dialogue between the police juvenile liaison officer and the education welfare officer on the panel:

Juvenile Liaison Officer: 'This lad is two brain cells below dead. His father has been inside prison for four years for indecency with his daughter. The older brother is also serving eighteen months. Mother is unable to read or write. The family has got money problems, and there's no electricity in the house. The whole situation is appalling really.'

EWO: 'The mother has asked me to give her a lift to the police station. I know she's pregnant, but it's

	difficult for me to stay on after work until six to take her to the police station.'
Juvenile Liaison Officer:	'I think she just can't be bothered. It's their responsibility to turn up for the caution. The police don't have the time to mess around with these families.'
EWO:	'Anyway, the mother shouldn't have difficulty in taking a bus.' (Grey Division)

The discussion ended with the youth and community worker protesting softly, 'It would be a shame to take him to court for such minor theft.' Although it seemed clear to all the social agencies that the mother had to cope with extreme poverty and the associated problems of having two family members in prison, they had to work within the constraints of the administrative distinction between 'cooperative' and 'uncooperative' clients.

The orientation of the cautioning authority to screen for a less troubled class of delinquents means that young people and their families have to adhere to a set of rules, not simply crime-related rules, but rules about keeping appointments, displaying parental concern and family discipline. Furthermore, putting the young people and their parents to inconvenience is in itself a compromise with retribution within a pre-court framework. As the police juvenile liaison officer in Red Division put it, 'If their child has offended, they should be made to come to the station at the designated time on the specified date. We're here to drive home the unacceptability of the offending behaviour, not to make life easy for them.' Indeed, parental responsibility was a theme of Conservative administrations in the 1980s and 1990s.[1] The broad thrust of Thatcher governments in 'rolling back the state' had, as one of its corollaries, the replacement of public and state activity by 'personal choice' and family activity. Yet, subsequent criminal justice legislations operated on the basis that 'responsible' behaviour can only be promoted by punishing the parents of young people in trouble. This is clearly one of the central arguments behind the White Paper, *Crime, Justice and Protecting the Public* (1990a), with its unpopular and unsuccessful proposal to hold parents responsible for actions committed by children under ten. In the event, parental responsibility is enforced under the 1991 Criminal Justice Act through its emphasis on compulsory parental attendance at court and making parents responsible for payment of fines, and the new power of the youth court to bind over the parents. The combined effect of these changes is to publicly 'implicate parents in the criminality of their children by requiring them to take their place alongside their child in court' (Edwards, 1992, p.117). As we shall see in Chapter 6, these moral assumptions about parental (ir)responsibility are equally valid in the administration of police cautioning.

DISCUSSION

The police have developed, historically, considerable freedom of action in the treatment of juvenile delinquents and their families. To the extent that cautioning is seen as an extension of the contable's common law discretion, there is an asymmetry of power between social agencies and the police. This raises fundamental questions about the possibilities and limitations of multi-agency consultation. In order to influence individual case disposal, social agencies always need to be perceived as within the bounds of existing conventions: they must be seen as objective, realistic and grounded in common sense with all the connotations this carries for interpreting juvenile offending. An occasional gain in terms of placing a young person on the cautioning side of the pre-prosecution tariff is made at the expense of longer-term conformity. Any panel member who then breaks the tacit agreement can be discounted by the police – the recommendations 'pushed to one side'. The end result of credibility-building by social agencies leads to a fine line between coming up with a 'realistic' decision and simply reinforcing the police tendency to 'push-in' very minor offences which, had they been committed by adults, would be regarded as 'rubbish' (McConville et al., 1991) by the police.

There is an alternative to the case-by-case review approach, which involves highlighting the young people's experience of crime and policing. To give one example: at the time of research, there was allegedly a recorded 300 per cent increase in street robberies, according to the police statistics in Blue Division. Rather than taking such statistics at face value, the social services representatives highlighted the racial dimension in what the young people themselves described as the 'taxing and bullying' in the streets. By raising the issue of racial attacks and harassment of black youth in town centres, the social services representatives were able to go some way in highlighting the gap between the police's understanding of street crime and the lived realities of some residents in a multi-racial locality. As Loader (1996, p.50) has argued, young people make use of 'public' space (e.g. on street corners, in local parks, city centres and shopping malls) more than any other social group because of their exclusion from autonomous private spaces and cultural resources – 'having nowhere to go, nothing to do, no money to spend'. The regular use of public space has, in turn, shaped young people's adversarial experiences of overpolicing and as victims of crime. Clearly, a lot more needs to be done on the part of these social agencies to address wider issues pertinent to the relationship between young people and police authority. Rather than legitimizing the police targeting of particular areas in city centres as problematic, social agencies in multi-agency settings can reflect the everyday realities of young people living in an increasingly segregated and hostile urban environment.

Whilst this research study has confirmed the power differential between police and non-police agencies, with the police claiming a special place in the definition of events and case construction, there are problems with lumping together the probation service, social services and education welfare service as sharing the same political and ideological positions about social policy. Social agencies may have different perceptions of the problem of juvenile delinquency; the legitimacy of their perceptions may vary according to their position within the hierarchy of professions. The next chapter looks at the relations between agencies, and how tensions between them may affect the outcomes of multi-agency negotiation.

5 Conflicts in Multi-Agency Liaison

Despite the generalized consensus in multi-agency forums that juvenile delinquency is a 'problem', it does not necessarily mean the same thing to the different agencies involved in caution decision-making. Police and social agencies have their own 'theories' as to the origins of the problem, while basing their responses on different assumptions as to what should be done in practical terms. This is not unique to multi-agency work with young people. In their research into inter-organizational perspectives on alcohol-related problems, Friend and others (1981) found that the ways in which different professional groupings perceived and responded to alcohol problems were mediated by factors such as their routine of work and occupational cultures. Hence, whereas social workers typically met alcohol-related problems in the form of child neglect, domestic difficulties and housing problems, the police generally dealt with such problems in the context of public disorder, household disturbances and road traffic offences. General practitioners, on the other hand, spent very little time with declared alcohol problems, and when they did they were typically associated with physical ailments and illnesses. This chapter looks at how agencies' understanding of, and responses to, juvenile delinquency are shaped by their position within a hierarchy of professions, which in turn affect the dynamics and outcome of multi-agency consultation.

WHOSE PROBLEM IS IT ANYWAY?

I begin with the relations between the probation service and social services within the youth justice system. The way that probation services and local authority social services departments have carved out different client groups within the criminal justice system can be traced back to the legislative changes in the

1960s. As Harris and Webb (1984) have argued, one of the intentions of the 1969 Children and Young Persons Act was to effect the transfer of responsibility for most young offenders from probation services to social services so that social services would have predominant responsibility for juvenile delinquents and children dealt with under the court's civil powers. Although the intention that probation's juvenile role should become altogether residual did not materialize, the dominant trend over the last two decades has been for the probation services to gradually reduce their involvement with juveniles, at first in practice and then later in policy terms (Bell and Haines, 1991).[1] This resulted in the bulk of work with juvenile offenders being undertaken by social services. The 'successful revolution in juvenile justice' in the 1980s is seen as largely brought about by juvenile justice specialists working in local authority social services departments, sometimes in collaboration with national or local voluntary organizations (Jones, 1988, 1993; Rutherford, 1992). The Children Act 1989 further strengthened the diversionary role of social services by making it a responsibility of local authorities 'to take reasonable steps designed to reduce the need to bring criminal proceedings against juveniles within their area'. This provides a framework for the development of services and support to young people who have been cautioned and to their families. With regard to the probation service, however, it has become firmly identified with the adult criminal justice system through its role in delivering 'punishment in the community' (Home Office, 1988, 1995; May, 1991; Vass, 1989; McWilliams, 1992). In a future envisaged by the 1988 Green Paper *Punishment, Custody and Community*, and the 1991 Criminal Justice Act, the probation service has a 'centre stage' position within the criminal justice system. In practice, tensions are rife between the probation service and the Home Office (and between probation management and main grade officers), as the probation service is increasingly called upon by the government to strengthen the enforcement of community penalties and to demonstrate that 'the probation service is in business to attack crime' (HM Inspectorate of Probation, 1993, p.42). Pressure on the service to comply with the government's vision of probation as a 'community correctional service' has also been maintained by the increasing involvement of private companies and voluntary organizations in supervising offenders in the community and, more recently, the abolition of social work qualifications and the proposal to recruit ex-army and ex-police officers into the probation service.

The introduction of the youth court and the provision of community sentences for sixteen- and seventeen-year-olds brought further changes to the de facto 'division of labour' between probation and social services. Under the 1991 Criminal Justice Act, probation and social services are required formally to share responsibility for work with offenders aged under eighteen and to agree structures and processes for the management of work with young offenders.[2] In principle, seventeen-year-olds were brought into the youth court jurisdiction so that they could benefit from the welfare philosophy in juvenile justice. A multi- agency approach for working with young offenders is to be adopted at the policy development and strategic management level. Similarly, at the operational level, allocation of responsibility for supervising sixteen- and seventeen-year-olds under the Criminal Justice Act 1991 is to be decided through multi-agency negotiations with reference to local circumstances.[3] In practice, there has been 'a lack of clarity and consensus nationally, whether, and if so, how far work with young offenders should be differentiated from work with adults' (Inspectorate of Probation, 1994, p.23).

This dual agency responsibility left much room for rivalry between agencies even before the 1991 Criminal Justice Act. In Red Division the 'battle for clients' between the probation and social services intensified, as one social services team leader put it, because of a widening gap in the distribution of local resources:

'The probation service don't have the time and resources that I have, and there's some very, very serious gap here. They say, "You don't realize the pressure we're under, we don't have the crew, we don't have the time to do home visits, we don't have the resources to do supported cautions." Well, my team will do it then. Give us the file, and we'll do it.'

(Social services team leader, Red Division)

In Red Division the perceived threat from the social services juvenile justice teams became particularly acute when they were given the local responsibility to supervise all sixteen-year-olds and under for court imposed supervision orders. The probation services were described by the education welfare officer in the JJB as 'fighting to keep their juvenile clients, their juvenile role, like crazy'. Even the senior probation officer admitted:

'The social services juvenile justice section in [Red Division] has become so big and so strong that we don't have juvenile clients now. At one time we used to work a lot with juveniles. Now we don't because the social services work with them.'
(Senior probation officer, Red Division)

These feelings of legitimate territory being invaded were also apparent in disagreement over the issue of home visits. At the time of research, routine home visits were conducted only in Red Division, either by social services or the probation service. In the other three localities, information might be forthcoming if, by chance, the juveniles or their family were already a client of social services. That probation officers in Red Division (and to a lesser degree in Yellow Division) were now opposed to home visits on every juvenile brought before the Bureau was perceived by social services, as well as the education welfare service, less as a sign of concern over the invasion of privacy (as the senior probation officer in Red Division would argue) than as an attempt to restrict the role of social services.

What is perhaps ironic is that conflict can also manifest itself in a rigid demarcation of 'whose problem is this?' In deciding which agency would conduct a home visit, for instance, social agencies would sometimes go out of their way to reinforce a rigid ownership of the 'problem' based on the age of the juvenile. Whilst this can have the inclusionary effect of safeguarding the influence of the less powerful agencies, a rigid demarcation may also have an exclusionary effect of allowing agencies to pull out from any claim that someone is 'their' problem. When rigid rules of ownership are taken to the extreme, bizarre situations may arise. To give one example: M, aged 13 years and 11 months, was charged with shoplifting in December, but because of the delay in processing files over the Christmas holidays his case was only brought before the juvenile liaison bureau in March the following year. By then M was already fourteen years of age, and the agencies were confused as to 'whose problem he is':

Social Services: 'He is not our responsibility. We don't necessarily pick him up if he's homeless. He's not on income support and he's never been in care.'

Probation: 'He's technically not our responsibility either. I'm afraid there has been some confusion regarding his age here on my file.'

After five minutes of discussion about whether a probation officer or a social worker should do the home visit, the education welfare officer joined in:

EWO: 'He was suspended and left school six months ago, so we won't have anything on him.' (Yellow Division)

Indeed, such artificial distinction of client groups may bear no relationship to the problems young people face in contemporary society. For young people do not live their lives conveniently parcelled up into any neat institutional boundaries; and it is often in the spaces between them that the issue of juvenile offending has to be confronted. When faced with situations that they cannot locate within their domains, professionals may become paralysed and unable to act.

THE EDUCATION WELFARE SERVICE

The power differential in multi-agency consultation is also apparent when we consider the role of the education welfare service. At the time of research, school reports were routinely presented by the senior education welfare officer to the liaison forum in Red Division; in others, school information was referred to on an ad hoc basis, for instance, when the juvenile was already known to the education welfare service. School information presented by education welfare officers typically includes information on attendance, academic ability and achievement, attitudes to school work and assessment of the pupil's character and behaviour, which often shades off into disciplinary issues. Comments ranged from the relatively mild:

> 'Attitude to work is variable; casual approach to school work; works hard when she enjoys the task; never really liked school even in her early days.'
> 'Completes tasks on time; generally well-behaved but likes to show off.'
> 'Difficult at school, but helpful with teachers at times; needs a more positive approach to study if he wants to lead a good life.'
> 'Keen to respond to questions; generally quite polite but impulsive; problems with rules of school uniform.'

to the more damaging:

> 'Low academic ability; incidents of confrontation with authority during lunch breaks; background leads him to see little value in education.'
> 'Lacks self discipline; behaviour seems inconsistent; at times eager to please and behave, at times his objective seems to be to entertain and amuse classmates, parents would come up with excuses for every act of his stupidity and carelessness.'
> 'Habitual truant. Hangs around with undesirable peers; easily-led; poorly motivated; disinterested in studies; often very disruptive, creates restlessness in school, can be a catalyst.'
> 'Avoids work whenever possible.'

School information can also include an assessment of the parents, especially their attitudes to child discipline and to the school authority. Whilst behavioural problems at school may be explained away as 'just boys being boys', they can be reinterpreted as a sign of more serious trouble when parents fail to show appropriate concern over this 'drifting away'. Less than one-quarter of the school reports read out in the JLB in Red Division referred to some form of 'parental support':

> 'Mom phoned up saying the child has had problems with his homework; school thinks that is a positive move.'
> 'Parents' attitudes to the juvenile's misbehaviour in school are solid and disapproving.'
> 'Parents fully on our side; they show interest in attending our school meetings.'

Because school authority's assessments of problematic parents are tied up with the professional ideologies and exigencies of practice within a school context, conflicts arise when the police and other agencies perceive the problem and the solution differently. The following example illustrates this. In this case, D (male, 15 years of age) was charged with handling a stolen bicycle. Given his two previous cautions for assault charges, the police chairman was noticeably reluctant to 'let him off' again this time:

> EWO: 'He has got 80 per cent attendance which is quite good. He is a classic underachiever and will only work if pushed, but he won't try his best. The school report here also says he can be quite immature. With some form of structure, he can behave reasonably well. He tries to get attention in class, and behaves like a clown.'

After almost five minutes of negative comments of this type, the police chairman turned to the senior probation officer and asked her what she knew about D. The senior probation officer then remarked that D came from a 'supportive family', and that if he could get a job in the future he could keep away from trouble.

EWO: 'My report here says there is no support from parents whatsoever. They don't turn up for meetings. There has been no contact with parents in spite of a great deal of input by education welfare service and the schools to try to get the youngster back to school. So I don't know where the "supportive family" bit comes from.'

SPO: 'Well, the father was there during the whole interview. When the mother couldn't make the first appointment, she wrote to us to explain, so she did make an effort. So perhaps the school did not offer enough appointments.'

EWO: 'Oh, we did, believe me!'   (Yellow Division)

The unsuccessful attempt of the school to get the parents involved often creates an impression that 'something has to be done'. But as Sheila Brown (1991) has suggested, 'parental involvement' is not a neutral term. Instead, it is based on a middle-class notion of the appropriate relationship between schools and 'interested' parents and a conception of family pathology: that is, that 'problematic' students generally tend to come from 'disorganised' or 'irresponsible' families. This definitional process is in turn contingent upon the practical exigencies of agency practice which, in the above example, may be conflicting and precarious in nature. Given the high case-load of education welfare officers and the simple necessity to work out a rough and ready way of identifying individual or family pathology based on one or more interviews, assessments often become dominated by bureaucratic concerns – such as securing the attendance of parents at interviews or a letter explaining their non-attendance. Or in another case where the parents were divorced, the fact that the father dropped by during the officer's home visit (only to collect his mail) was described as 'a sign of parental concern' in the education welfare officer's plea for a police caution.

THE HIERARCHIES OF KNOWLEDGE

Despite the significant overlapping of interests between the education welfare service and the police over disciplinary issues, education welfare officers clearly have the least power in terms of influencing the case outcomes. This echoes the research findings of Macmillan (1991), who found that whilst the schools' adverse views did not necessarily affect panel decisions and appeared sometimes to be discounted, 'there were instances when the panels, in the absence of other information, were swayed by the views presented'. On the other hand, positive control indicators in the school report alone would not sway the decision. This relates to the way that the police make use of school information in their decision-making process. School information on family only becomes relevant when it reinforces the police's moral assessment – for instance, the parents' attitudes towards the offence ('I was very concerned about the sheer lack of concern or condemnation by the parents') or attitudes towards the police themselves ('parents extremely helpful with the enquiries'). School information may also be considered useful to the extent it provides pointers of the likelihood of the family cooperating with the police in disciplining the offender and instilling into the child the appropriate sentiments of remorse and regret. As we shall see in the next chapter, this is a key issue in the administration of cautioning. At the same time, however, the police are also aware of the limited relevance of school information to the specific offence in question. Hence the many occasions when the education welfare officer's opinion was passed over in meetings:

'Behaviour in school is different from behaviour outside. But it's nice to have those little extra bits; it shows we're not making decisions lightly.'

(Police chairman of JJB, Red Division)

The only exception is when truancy becomes highlighted in the school report as a problem. On these occasions, alliances can be formed between the education welfare service and the police in pushing school attendance as a key issue for caution decision-making:

> 'What is support from parents? It is an offence not to have a youngster in school, and therefore parents should see to it that their youngsters are fully educated. When a lad has been out of school and his parents have not tried to get him back to school despite all our help, that's not support from parents in my view.'   (Education welfare officer, Yellow Division)

The historically central tasks of the education welfare service of policing (to enforce regular school attendance) and welfare (a concern for the school student's 'social, medical and nutrition needs') are significant (Wardhaugh, 1990, p.738). Here, one is reminded of the traditional image of education welfare officers as school attendance officers or 'child snatchers'. Against the background of the Puritan work ethic and a new urban industrial order in the late nineteenth century, a more systematically trained and disciplined workforce was required to implement the fundamental social and economic changes. The nature and manner of provision of education was to become central to the transformation of disciplined children to disciplined workers. It was the acceptance of universal and regular schooling as the normal, indeed the only possible, pattern of schooling on which the education welfare service was based (Carlen et al., 1992; Macmillan, 1977). Along with the definition of regular schooling as 'normal' comes the pathologization of absence from school as 'deviant'. Within a range of education research and criminological and social science literature, truancy has been seen as a sign of individual pathology, a sign that the child is drifting, in trouble, and not under control (cf. Paterson, 1989; Reid and Kendall, 1982). From a policing point of view, any unstructured, unsupervised and essentially 'disorganized' inactivity by young people is potentially threatening and all too close to other forms of law-breaking. This assumption that enforcing school attendance will bring about order as well as educational benefits is crucial to the development of police truancy patrol. Despite the lack of conclusive evidence that truancy patrols can safeguard young people from involvement in criminal activities or protect them from moral danger, police truancy patrols enjoyed a considerable degree of popularity during the late 1980s, and at one stage were conducted jointly with the education welfare services in areas such as Bedfordshire and Birmingham (Carlen et al., 1992).

This pathology of truancy, however, is not necessarily shared by other social agencies. Social workers and probation officers can be reluctant to distinguish between 'deserving' and 'undeserving' students. Hence their argument that a young person's behaviour in school, relationships with teachers and peers and so on, should be irrelevant to caution decisions. The fear is that juveniles could be 'prosecuted because of a bad school report':

'You see, we have switched from welfare issues to justice issues, which now makes school reports less relevant. The previous education welfare officer used to read it all out; he always said "Do you want to hear what's in the school report?" And quite frankly, the Bureau has progressed to such a stage that we didn't really need to hear what's in the school report. It wouldn't add or subtract anything to the decision we've made. But we used to allow him to go through the formality anyway.
(Senior probation officer, Yellow Division)

'I don't think education welfare input can be necessarily in the young person's best interests, particularly since school information can often be very negative. These are young offenders and kids who cause trouble, they might well have done the same in school. The schools will inevitably be biased against the young person.
(Social services team leader, Red Division)

In other words, education welfare is perceived by other social agencies as the remnants of a discredited welfare approach under which 'youngsters could be punished and brought to court for the wrong reasons', as the manager of the Community Services Centre in Blue Division put it. Effective constraints or guidelines on the content of school reports may ameliorate some of the worst examples of character assassination in school reports. But what is more pertinent to our understanding of multi-agency consultation is that 'partnership' can be more rhetorical than real, as it masks some significant hierarchies of knowledge. The differential perceptions of what diversion is all about is simply one example of many such differences between social agencies: each has its own organizational philosophy, perception of the value of other services and typology of delinquents. Carlen and others (1992) pointed out that education welfare officers are often accused of 'not knowing their place' and, therefore, jeopardizing the work of 'real' professionals. What is alarming is that even when agencies admit that education welfare input may *not* be in the 'best interests' of the juvenile, the ideology of 'working together' dictates the mandate of juvenile liaison, and multi-agency consultation becomes merely a token gesture to improve relations between managers.

Most education welfare officers in the research study were not unaware of the lack of 'fit' between education welfare work and the offence orientation in policework:

'I feel we should be concerned with consideration of the offence and not really the other aspects of the juvenile and circumstances; to my mind, his behaviour at school is not so relevant to issues of justice, not as relevant as his previous convictions and offending behaviour... It does put the education welfare representative in a dilemma really. Having said that I support the view of a justice model rather than welfare considerations, so what am I actually doing here?'

(Divisional manager, education welfare service,
Yellow Division)

This disjuncture partly accounts for the sense of alienation or ambivalence among education welfare officers observed in the research study. This is how one education welfare officer struggled to justify the relevance of school information to decisions of cautioning:

'If you get... like social development... we have on our form something like attitude to school work, and that gives you some idea whether the youngster is going to go on and do GCE, or do work or how good he is at it; maybe he is performing very well in work experience and to go to court would jeopardize his future. And that would have a bearing. Then we have behaviour and relationships in school. If in school, he's never... if he's been very polite to the teachers, if he or she has very good relationships with other pupils, it might have a bearing on what he has done outside, or it might not. (Team leader, education welfare service, Red Division)

In response, educational welfare officers routinely distinguished between schools which were 'helpful' or 'objective' and those which were 'vindictive', i.e. only interested in getting rid of their 'troublesome' students:

'There have been times a school has already known about the offence. Sometimes they look for incidents to fit, to make it a stronger case. Perhaps they feel this student should be prosecuted; they kind of look for evidence to fit that.'

(Senior EWO, Grey Division)

'I think many schools think we're too kind to the youngsters. They do see the JLB as a vehicle to punish the youngsters.'
(Principal EWO, Blue Division)

'Sometimes, the school would try to put pressures on us, to use the opportunity to punish the juveniles, and to bring them to court.'

(Team leader, education welfare service, Red Division)

This belief that some schools could be biased and looking for incidents to fit the case for prosecution is a theme constantly raised by education welfare officers in the research study. But instead of challenging the relevance of school information per se, they routinely resorted to a filtering strategy – 'not change a report, but leave some information out', in the words of one education welfare officer. Hence anecdotal information could be skimmed over or school reports cut short:

'I'd be looking at the information I've been given, and I'd be selective as to what I actually tell the Bureau. I wouldn't be reading out the whole report. It's difficult to say what specific information you should give to the Bureau to enable a just decision to be made. But if you give too much or just the wrongs of the juvenile, you know very well that if you come clean, the juvenile would be dragged into the justice system.'
(Senior education welfare officer, Grey Division)

This sifting process is important, as the ability to distinguish the 'vindictive' comment from what is 'negative' but 'fair' is seen as a key site of neutral, professional judgements. The craft of sifting is regarded as an esoteric one, acquired through the experience of mediating between the young people, parents and schools, and involving a specific form of knowledge and expertise unavailable to others. Education welfare officers in the research study typically remark that school information has to be reinterpreted in the light of individual circumstances. In effect, this ideology of professionalism precludes any questioning of the personal judgements of education welfare officers either by schools (because the schools are partial), by other juvenile justice specialists in the multi-agency forum (because they do not have the detailed facts of each case), or by the juveniles and their parents (because unlike school reports in court, their contents are not disclosed to the 'defence' in the pre-court stage).

Within a bureaucratic structure of juvenile liaison, tensions between agencies may sometimes serve to clarify and specify their different professional roles. By challenging other agencies' perceptions of problems and priorities, inter-agency conflicts may actually put all agencies 'on the spot' and make them more accountable for their judgements and decisions. Hughes and others (1995, p.11) have argued that in areas such as Northamptonshire, where multi-agency liaison staff may be 'battle-hardened' about the dangers of 'administrative justice ... behind closed doors', multi-agency consultation may have greater potential in policing the boundaries of the local criminal justice system. Potential pitfalls in operating within an assumption of 'professional-managerial consensus' in multi-agency consultation nevertheless remain. Blagg and Smith (1989, p.41) have warned of the dangers involved when 'juvenile liaison panels engage in gratuitous gossip about particular children which... tended to establish the child as a "problem" for the agencies and made him or her "someone to be watched"'. Multi-agency decisions are often overlaid by an administrative concern with ensuring the smooth flow of business so that even the most transparently manipulative construction of cautionable cases can be represented as being 'in the child's best interests'. That the young people and their families do not necessarily perceive cautioning as being 'in their best interests' is the main concern in the next chapter.

6 Receiving Police Cautioning

To date there has been no systematic research on the experience of police cautioning from the viewpoint of the young people and their families. In a welfarist rhetoric, young people are given a police caution – a second chance – rather than being sucked into the formal court system. The notion of progress in pre-court diversion is often underlined by its claim to remove children from the criminalizing ethos of the court and the potentially damaging effects of stigmatization and labelling. Furthermore, there is an implicit assumption that the informal handling of delinquents (as in the Scottish Children Hearings System) may promote parental involvement and a sense of partnership between the state and the parents of offending children (National Youth Agency, 1991; NACRO, 1994). In practice, does police cautioning really represent an alternative to court? Or has it simply altered the place and meaning of punishment in the criminal justice system? Do young people and their parents regard police cautioning as a 'soft option', as critics in favour of giving cautioning 'some teeth' often claim? Do they accept the service role of the police in preventing young people from getting into trouble? This chapter seeks to address these questions by drawing on observations of police cautioning sessions and a series of interviews with the police, and those juveniles and their parents who received a caution at the station.

THE APPROPRIATE ADULT

The Police and Criminal Evidence Act (PACE) 1984 and its accompanying Codes of Practice (revised in 1995) lay out specific requirements to be placed upon the police, and set out the rights of a suspect. In particular, they provide the right to free legal advice and to notification for any person detained in custody at a police station. In the case of a juvenile (and the mentally ill or handicapped), an 'appropriate adult' must be informed of his or her detention by the custody officer and asked to attend the station. For juveniles, the adult will usually be a parent but can also be a guardian, a social worker or other 'responsible adult'. In principle, the main tasks of the appropriate adult are to ensure that the interview is conducted fairly, to ensure that the young person's rights are complied with and, where necessary, to facilitate communication. It is, however, meaningless to refer to these rules as 'rights' in the abstract (Association for Juvenile Justice, 1990). Although all the parents and care workers in the research study said that they knew they had a right to legal advice, none sought legal advice during the police interview. The majority of juveniles and parents gave triviality of the offence ('because I know it's only a minor offence'; 'having a solicitor might complicate things'), the fact that the offence was the first committed by the juvenile ('because he's never been in trouble before'), or the guilt of the juvenile ('I did it, I'm not denying that') as the main reasons for deciding not to seek legal advice. Such findings seem to confirm the main reasons given for not seeking legal advice in previous studies (Morris and Giller, 1977; Evans, 1993d). However, assessments of the 'trivial' nature of the offence (and hence not worth seeking legal advice) are often contingent upon the attitude of the interviewing officers and their off-the-record reassurances that the offence is not something 'serious' (see also Sanders and Bridges, 1990; Evans, 1996).[1] In practice, there may be a very thin line between reassuring the juveniles and parents that it is in their 'best interests' to avoid a court appearance and pressurizing the juvenile to admit the offence. Parents in the research study were unsure at which point such reassurances were made – before, during or after the formal interview. But what is significant is that the majority of parents had the distinct impression from the interviewing officers that a caution was 'just a simple procedure': 'We thought the thing to do was to cooperate with police enquiries and be helpful', as one parent put it.

What constitutes cooperation with the police is a problematic issue, however. Whilst the Codes of Practice insist that the role of the appropriate adult is not a passive one, and that the appropriate adult is not expected to act simply as an observer, there is evidence to suggest that the police might expect just that. Parents who take an active stance and interrupt the police interview can attract police hostility. In the following case of arson (setting fire to an athletics equipment store), the parent of R (aged 13) was denounced as 'uncooperative' in the police file. Such assessment was then passed on to the Juvenile Liaison Panel as part of the background information. The police interview notes give us an idea of the basis for the assessment:

Police officer: 'Everyone else is saying that you are responsible. They've detailed exactly how you're responsible, so would you care to take this opportunity without me badgering it out of you, to say exactly what your involvement was?'

R made no reply and looked over to father.

Father: 'I wish the tape to be stopped and I advise [my son] to say no more until we consult our solicitor. Thank you.'

Police officer: 'You need not make any comment at this stage, if you require a duty solicitor present this could be arranged.'

Father: 'No, we will listen to the statement, as I say, we will make no comment unless my son is charged with this. I will consult a solicitor, I'll wait until then.' (Blue Division)

Holdaway (1983) argued that the active presence of parents and social workers may be seen as 'a challenge' on police territory as it threatens the smooth running of the system.[2] One of the stated intentions of requiring the presence of an 'appropriate adult' where a juvenile is interviewed is to ensure that the interview is conducted fairly. This implies a certain degree of understanding of what constitutes 'fair' proceedings, acceptable interviewing techniques and proper questions to be asked which, according to Evans (1993d), cannot be taken for granted. Parents, guardians or even social workers may be unsure of their exact role: do they advise the young person, or simply observe the proceedings? In terms of who should act as the 'appropriate adult', some have suggested that the police prefer social workers, with their rough idea of correct procedures, compared to parents who might be unduly obstructive (Sandell, 1992). Others have argued the opposite, that parents are the preferred option precisely because they have less idea of the procedures (Blackwell, 1990). Research commissioned by the 1993 Royal Commission on Criminal Justice tends to support the latter argument, not least because it found parents – who made up 80 per cent of the 'appropriate adults' – only too willing to assist the police in obtaining improper confessions (Evans, 1993d). And the result? Instead of opening up the closed world of the police station, the 'appropriate adult' may merely act as an adjunct to the authority of the police, a compliant condoner of poor police practice, or a 'stimulant for a whole range of threats and hostilities from the police' (Thomas, 1988).[3]

PARENTAL RESPONSIBILITY AND CONTROL

Whilst police officers in the research study stressed that it is important for parents to be present at interviewing and cautioning sessions, the importance seems to be related not so much to legal considerations as to their search for control indicators. In other words, the presence of the parents at police stations serves a function quite different from those stated under PACE:

> 'The parents' attitude is as important as the juvenile's attitude. You do get a feeling whether parents are supportive or anti-authority.'   (Cautioning Inspector, Grey Division)

> 'You want to know what the parents think of the offence, and what they're going to do about it.'
>
>   (Cautioning Inspector, Blue Division)

Police officers administering the caution have a distinct image of the 'irresponsible poor' – getting drunk, smoking and going to the bingo three times a week, spending money on luxurious items such as the video, not knowing the whereabouts of their offspring, failure to get children to school. This emphasis on the perceived home background – in terms of the moral character of parents, the level of parental (ir)responsibility and control over their children – seems to stem from a general belief that, when young people offend, the criminal justice system has a part to play in reminding parents of their responsibility. Police Inspectors in the study suggested that the reaction of parents at the caution session constituted a reliable gauge of the chances of reoffending – 'If they showed a couldn't care less attitude, then you can almost put your money on that juvenile would reoffend.' Questions of discipline and punishment were routinely put to the parents. In practice, even token gestures – such as cutting off the child's pocket money, grounding the child for a few nights, or removing the television set from his/her room – were readily accepted as signs of caring, and perhaps more importantly, cooperative parents.

Some parents admitted that they felt very uneasy about those questions on home background; some clearly felt the home situation had nothing to do with the specific offence. Some of these parents, however, went on to suggest that they felt it was part of a police strategy to punish them for their child's offence. They talked about feeling degraded and belittled before the police, an impression that the police were 'trying to bring you down':

'I think they tried to embarrass you, or make you feel ashamed of your son's behaviour, as if you're the one who committed the crime.'

(Interview with mother, Yellow Division)

'The way he said to my son, "It's disgraceful on your part to have your dad dragged down to the police station, he has done nothing wrong." I mean, that would only make me feel worse, wouldn't it?'   (Interview with father, Red Division)

As we shall see in the next section, cautioning sessions serve a function akin to that of a 'degradation ceremony' (Garfinkel, 1956), and any degrading tactics can be directed towards the parents as much as the juveniles. Furthermore, the police who were interviewed were clearly interested in the parents' own ability to comply with regulations and values of respect for property and authority figures. The images of wilfully negligent parents and criminogenic parents colluding with or even commanding their offsprings' delinquent behaviour were frequently alluded to. In particular, parents who objected to a caution (none in this study) could be criticized not only as uncooperative but also as having an 'attitude problem':

> 'Sometimes they come in here and sit there, look around or read a leaflet, and they just don't care. Some parents don't accept a caution. They think their son or daughter is not guilty of any offence.'
>
> (Cautioning Inspector, Yellow Division)

> 'Many parents have an attitude problem. They think it's no big deal, and they walk out saying that to the kid. So what kind of an impact would a caution have?'
>
> (Cautioning Inspector, Yellow Division)

> 'No, we don't get many parents objecting to a caution, touch wood. Some parents want their children to be brought to court to teach them a lesson; they do not care what is going to happen to their children.'
>
> (Cautioning Inspector, Blue Division)

THE CAUTIONING ENVIRONMENT

In principle, the cautioning process facilitates and encourages a police 'partnership' not only with other non-police agencies but also with the parents of offending children. In practice, the specific environment in which cautioning takes place is under the authority of, and strictly controlled by, the police. This is a significant part of the police tactics. The managers of social agencies in multi-agency forum played no role in the cautioning sessions. Apart from their senior rank (usually an Inspector), male police officers who administered the cautioning were not chosen on the basis of any special qualifications or training. Instead, the mere fact that an Inspector has children of his own could be seen as a good enough reason to put him in charge of cautioning. Although these senior officers argued that different officers have their own style of administering a caution, they were keen to elaborate on their stock-in-trade tactics of how to achieve the greatest impact on the juveniles and parents:

> 'If they're crying you know you're getting through. You need to shake them up, but you don't need to shout at everyone.'
>
> 'If it's a first-time offender, I'll sit on a chair, make him or her stand in front of me, parents behind so the child won't be distracted.'
>
> 'I use my body language, make the youngsters look at me, standing in front, and the parents sitting.'
>
> 'I'd force eye contact with them and say "Would you look at me when I'm talking to you?"'
>
> 'I used to talk to the parents first and make the youngster stand outside, like a headmaster.'
>
> 'I don't caution co-offenders together; kids tend to listen more attentively when they are on their own.'

This manipulation of the cautioning environment is akin to the manipulation of the interrogation environment which aims at, as police advice manuals often suggest, heightening the pressure upon the suspect and thereby increase the likelihood of a confession. Even the design and spatial layout of interview rooms can be manipulated, as McConville and others (1993, p.132) observed:

> ... there was an absence of aural and visual stimuli; the suspect's chair was relatively immobile, often, indeed, being fixed to the floor; the principal or dominant interviewer confronted the suspect directly, with the subordinate interviewer both

able to observe the suspect and have eye contact with the dominant interviewer...and the interviewers themselves were able to move their chairs around and, in particular, to close in on the suspect if necessary, and to facilitate this (and full visual assessment of the suspect), there was in general no table between suspect and interviewers.

The cautioning environment sets the stage for, and is an integral part of, the informal processing of troublesome youths. There is an implicit consensus among the multi-agency representatives in the research study that a caution should be administered sternly and strongly – 'as a screw is turned very tightly on them', as one social worker put it metaphorically. The routine administration of the caution takes as its reference point the court-based punishment paradigm but in a swift (for instance, no more than eight weeks after the commission of the offence), economical and direct manner (face-to-face with the police and without legal representation).

THE ADMINISTRATION OF A CAUTION

Not all Police Inspectors explained the caution decision, its status and implications (for instance, that it is citable in court) at the beginning of the cautioning session. In a few cases, the consent of the juvenile and parent was sought only towards the end of the session, almost as an afterthought. Whilst the majority of juveniles and parents claimed that they could follow the gist of what was being said to them, they tended to lack full comprehension. In particular, younger children found long words and legal terms alien. Some juveniles were at a loss when asked to sign the relevant form ('What is this for?'), and parents were confused ('What is its difference from a criminal record?'). Cautioning sessions were in the main occasions for the delivery of moral lectures. From the police point of view, a caution may include two main facets: a 'heart-to-heart talk' (unless, of course, the juvenile is seen as too delinquent to benefit from some friendly advice) and a stern 'dressing down'.

First, the 'heart-to-heart talk' covers almost invariably the adverse consequences of having a criminal record, such as difficulties in settling down, having a family, earning other people's trust and, most importantly, finding a job. Here, the main purpose is to point out to the young person 'the road he's heading down':

Inspector: 'You want to get a job in a few years' time, don't you? You won't get a job if you have a criminal record. If two people are applying for the job at the same time and one has a criminal record and the other doesn't, who do you think they'll employ? You?'
J: 'No.'   (Yellow Division)

This normative model of the transition from school to the labour market is premised on conditions of full employment and the traditional structures of industry which do not exist in contemporary Britain. It is common for young people to be unemployed for at least part of their post-school careers, especially the least qualified students who in the previous decades would have gone directly into low-skilled jobs on leaving school (Jones and Wallace, 1992). Critics have argued that the lack of employment and genuine training opportunities has hit young people with such a ferocity that many of them may remain outside the labour market permanently (Williamson, 1993). This is despite the state's 'training solution' to young people's disadvantages in the labour market through schemes such as the Youth Training Scheme (YTS) and the subsequent Youth Training (YT) (Raffe, 1991). Seen in this context, the police lecture on the moral value of a work ethic, respectability, stability (directed to children as young as thirteen years of age) and the importance of being integrated into the next generation of disciplined adult workers may bear little meaning to the living strategies and limited possibilities of many of the young people appearing before the police.

A second facet of the moral lecture is a 'dressing down' of the juvenile, which in turn is linked with the general philosophies that the police identify with in fulfilling what they define as their role in the adversarial system of criminal justice. These philosophies are essentially oppositional in character, marked by a reliance upon the use of police power and authority. The question of motive was almost inevitably the first or second question which the Inspector asked of a juvenile, and the one which a juvenile was least able to answer. Most juveniles either stayed silent or replied 'I don't know'. For whatever answer could be given, it seemed almost certain to appear unacceptable to the police ('because it looked fun'; 'just something to do'). As one parent put it,

> 'Some of the questions that the officer asked [my son], I think they were very difficult questions to answer. Like "Why did you do it?", I mean, with those kinds of questions, you can't really put a finger on why you did it, can you?'
>
> (Red Division)

Although questions of 'who did what, when and why?' were routinely put to the juveniles, they were not raised merely to confirm what happened or elicit new information from the individual.[4] Instead, the focus on individual culpability generally set the scene for police comments on the juvenile's disgrace to the parents, the school or even the whole community. Questions such as 'What do you feel about your responsibility?', 'What do you think you've learnt from this incident?', 'Do you know you have let down your parents?', 'Your parents trusted you. Why did you betray their trust?', were frequently directed at the juveniles. The police effort to bring down the juvenile is both a means and an end in itself. Not only is the visible impact regarded as an indicator of the appropriateness and effectiveness of a caution, but it is the *only* immediate punishment within the police's power. The moral lecture underlined the juvenile's status as a criminal and, as such, performs a symbolic function similar to that of the court system.

> Inspector: 'Why are you here in the first place?'
> P: 'I don't know.'
> Inspector: 'So why did you do it?' [staring into P's eyes]

P: 'Don't know.'

Inspector: 'What makes you think of getting into the locker and taking the watch?'

P: 'Don't know.' [very soft spoken]

Inspector: 'Speak up a bit. What were you going to do with the watch?'

P: 'I haven't thought about it really.'

Inspector: 'You stole something and you don't know what to do with it!'

P: 'I'll probably throw it away.'

Inspector: 'Other people would ask you questions about the watch, wouldn't they? So that makes you what?'

P: 'A thief.' [almost in tears]

Inspector: 'A thief, uh!' [visibly satisfied with the answer]

(Red Division)

This ceremonial 'stripping of a man of his dignity' as a prelude to judicial punishment in court has been thoroughly explicated and analysed by Garfinkel (1956). What the cautioning system has done is to reproduce and institutionalize the court-based degradation ceremony in the police station. In this sense, the magistrates are no longer the only – or even the key – moral condemners.

What is regarded as 'appropriate' behaviour at a cautioning session also seems to be tied up with particular assumptions about female and male juveniles. Some officers felt that despite the small number of girls processed into the justice system, the 'hard core' who are on a par with the serious male offenders (or what one Inspector called the 'hard bitch') could be more devious ('They cry and use that as a disguise') and more difficult to manage than their male counterparts ('They are more self-assured, more mature than boys, but also very surly'). Police Inspectors pointed out that they can only be sure a caution was appropriate when they can discern that the process of receiving it has made some immediate impact upon the juveniles (and perhaps the parents). This practical emphasis on visible impact – for instance, making a juvenile sweat – and its problematic implications for the management of girls echo the findings of

Loraine Gelsthorpe's research study (1989). Whilst girls who fail to visibly express their emotions or respect for authority can be labelled as 'surly' or 'cocky' (and perhaps less likely to be given a second caution by the same officer), those who do comply are also more likely than boys to be denounced as 'devious' (Gelsthorpe, 1989, pp. 105–6).

SYMBIOTIC RELATIONSHIP BETWEEN CAUTIONING AND THE COURT SYSTEM

In diverting young people from court, the police ultimately have to evoke the punitive images and sanctioning power of the formal court system to make 'a strong impact' on them. For one thing, the juvenile is invariably led to believe that prosecution has been in prospect – that he/she has had a narrow escape. Letters are sent out informing the juvenile and parents to come to the police station, but they are left in suspense regarding the cautioning decision. This is calculated to maximize the impact of a caution. The deliberate presentation of the prosecution decision as being balanced on a knife-edge could backfire, however, as the following example illustrates. In this case, P was accompanied by his local authority care worker. P seemed very nervous throughout the caution session and could not even remember his date of birth. He was only allowed to sit down after the Inspector had explained the caution decision and made them sign the relevant papers.

Inspector:	'What do you think would have happened to you if you hadn't been brought here to see me?'
P:	'Don't know.'
Care worker:	'To court.'
P:	'Yes, to court.'
Inspector:	'What do you think the judge would do to you then?'
P:	'They would punish me.'
Inspector:	'Yes, you'd be fined, you could be put on probation. What's the last thing they could do to you?'

P: 'Send me to prison.'

Inspector: 'Your case has been considered carefully and we think you're worth another chance. So this is what it is – your second chance. Nothing will happen to you after this if you behave yourself, alright? But the minute you do something wrong and you get caught, you'd be brought to court. Have you done something wrong before?'

P: 'Once before.'

Inspector: 'What was that about?' [surprised]

The Inspector was not aware of P's first caution in relation to a case of shoplifting and was visibly embarrassed. He then made one final attempt to conjure up the image of the prison as just round the corner.

Inspector: 'So this is your second cautioning then. You seemed to have cracked the system. Two second chances. You won't come here again if you offend next time, I can promise you that. You'll go to court for this and the last offence as well, you'll get sent away then.'   (Red Division)

Not all juveniles were able to comprehend the cautioning process. On two occasions, the child was obviously too young to understand what was going on. This did not escape the attention of the Police Inspector, who nevertheless insisted that a 'no further action' decision would not have been more appropriate because the 'evidence was there'. The following example illustrates the absurd or even bemusing result of the police tendency to push offences into the system which would have been considered too trivial had they been committed by adults. In this case, A (male, aged 10) was involved in what the police described as a 'shoplifting spree' with his three other friends and cousins. A's case was regarded by the police as a 'straightforward' cautionable case and hence not discussed in the multi-agency liaison forum. A's parents were both present at the cautioning session. A stood next to his mother, sucking his thumb and looking bewildered:

Inspector:	'Why are you here?'
A:	'Handling stolen goods.'
Inspector:	'Yes, but what does handling mean?'
A:	'Don't know.'
Inspector:	'So you don't know why you're here?'
Mother [aside]:	'Say you've been naughty.'

Finding himself unable to get a satisfactory response from the child, the Inspector then shifted towards other areas of control indicators.

Inspector:	'Is this the start of a criminal career, or just bad luck?'
A:	'Bad luck.' [still sucking his thumb and was told off by his mother].
Inspector:	'Do you have trouble with him at home?'
Father:	'No.'

Realizing the futility of delivering his standard lecture, the Inspector simply went through the motion of telling A not to get into trouble again and then made him sign the form. The mother asked A if he could spell his name correctly and added, 'Sometimes he forgets!'   (Grey Division).

JUSTICE, FAIRNESS AND PUNISHMENT

The majority of juveniles who were interviewed thought they were given a caution mainly because they had 'never been in trouble before' and/or because the offence was not too 'serious'. But as Parker and others (1981) have argued, such a neat conclusion negates 'the full complexity of the views of those subject to the juvenile justice process and the often bitter and problematic nature of their own experiences' (p.118). For instance, although juveniles in their study voiced a broad agreement in ranking the court's range of disposals, their negative personal experience in court, perceptions of authority figures, inappropriateness and severity of the sentence, and an awareness of police power to define and 'bump up' charges, all served to erode notions of juvenile justice as fairness.

There is another aspect of the 'full complexity of the views' of the young people that merits attention here. Juvenile offending, especially offences of assault, often occur as but one step in a protracted series of encounters or conflicts. Harry Blagg (1985) has made a similar point in relation to the difficulties involved in developing personal reparation as part of a diversionary strategy. This is particularly so in cases of fights between peers or bullying among schoolchildren, which may take place on a confused set of grounds and reasons; victims, offenders and bystanders all may carry some responsibility. Some of the cases in this research study involved a degree of physical violence between schoolchildren, peers at a youth club or in the neighbourhood. Young people who were interviewed mentioned either a long-standing dispute with the 'victim', having been 'set up', or a feeling that the 'victim' also shared part of the blame. In so far as the caution was presented by the police as an alternative to criminal proceedings, they felt relieved at not having to go to court. Nevertheless, they also showed signs of resentment for being held solely responsible for the offence: 'It's not just all me. Why should I be the only one told off by the police? But I'm not saying it's all him.' (Male juvenile, Grey Division.)

The police cautioning process is ultimately mediated by the complexity of such feelings and perceptions of the young people, all of which may serve to erode the notion of pre-court justice as fairness. The majority of young people in the research study had never been cautioned before and, therefore, did not really know what to expect. Some had picked up impressions from friends or from relatives. When asked to describe what they made of the cautioning session, and specifically how they felt and to what extent they thought the police were harsh or sympathetic towards them, the response was mixed. The majority of the young people regarded the purpose of a caution and the role of the Police Inspector in punitive terms, i.e. punishing them for what they have done. Although the majority of them perceived the cautioning process in a routine and matter-of-fact manner ('It's basically a telling-off.'; 'He's alright, just doing his job.'), others who were interviewed at the police station or who had been cautioned before responded in more emotive terms:

> 'It was awful. I feel I'm in such a mess. I won't get into trouble again. I don't want to come back to the police station.' [still in tears]   (Yellow Division)

> 'I thought it would be more frightening... Not actually shouting at me, but raising his voice.'   (Red Division)

> 'I think I've got off lightly. I thought he would be a lot stricter, a lot more yelling at me this time. I couldn't sleep last night, I was so worried. Really lucky of me.'   (Yellow Division)

> 'I was frightened... it wasn't what I had expected... Well, yes, a telling-off, but not like this. ('Like what?') The way he just stared at me, like he was angry.'   (Blue Division)

More importantly, what the young people think of the caution, what they expect, and whether they feel they are treated sympathetically or too harshly by the police, are all tied up with the relationship between the police and young people and their routine encounters on the streets. Hence they spoke not only of the cautioning Inspectors who 'stared' or 'looked down at me', but also the interviewing officers who 'kept me in the cell' or said 'something terrible would happen to me', the officers who had stopped and searched them on the streets – these are all authority figures who have more power over them and over the definitions of the situation:

> 'The police stopped me on the streets and asked me to empty my pockets. I asked the officer, "Could we do this in the house?" He said, "No, on the side of the streets." It's not fair; they could have searched me at the station. There were people passing by. I tried to tell him why I had a knife on me, but he wouldn't listen. No.'   (Yellow Division)

Or at the police station:

> 'I didn't have a watch, so I didn't know how long I had to
> wait for my parents to get there... perhaps an hour or two. I
> was really scared, all those tapes and things (i.e. tape re-
> corders). I've never seen them before.'   (Blue Division)

None of the young people who were interviewed expected or
considered the pre-court caution to be a 'heart-to-heart talk'.
This is broadly in line with other court-based research findings
which indicate that young offenders regard the judicial system's
prime task in terms of punishment and control rather than care
and treatment (Morris and Giller, 1977; Parker et al., 1981). In
one case, the female juveniles flatly rejected the helping role of
the police. With only four female juveniles included in this
research study, it is difficult to delve into the paternalistic
dimension of the police 'heart-to-heart talk' with girls. But in
this case, M (female, aged 15) set fire to a waste-paper basket,
was cautioned in the presence of her social worker, and proved
to be one of the 'unruly resources' that challenged the smooth
running of the session and the police's moral authority:

> Inspector: 'I know you've been treated heavy-handedly in
>   the past. If only you would let me help you. We
>   don't want to keep hassling you.'
> M: 'How can you help me then?'
> Inspector: 'You tell me, love.'
> M: 'You can't help me. I can only help myself.
>   Nobody can. I've got my own mates. Nobody
>   can tell me not to do this, not to do that. I am
>   in charge of my own life.'   (Grey Division)

A SOFT OPTION?

Similarly, the majority of parents did not look to the police to
provide help and guidance for their children. Almost all of them
wanted the caution to be 'over and done with in one day'. In

particular, the parents were sceptical of getting involved with the social services, partly because of their perceptions of social workers as 'do-gooders' or 'child-snatchers' and partly because of the way they perceived the offence itself:

> 'I can't see how bringing in the social services would help actually. Because in a case like this, it has nothing to do with the way we bring up our kids or anything like that. It was only a spur of a moment thing, my son did something stupid and that was it.'
>
> (Interview with mother, Grey Division)

Only one parent suggested to me that some follow-up work by the youth and community services could keep his son in line. The majority of them also described the purpose of a caution in terms of a 'telling-off' or 'teaching the child a lesson'; some even expected harsher words from the police:

> ML: 'What do you think of the caution just now?'
> Father: 'I thought it would be harsher than that. No, not taking him to court, but a good telling off. Similar sort of, er... not atmosphere, but similar sort of situation if you went to court, but not actually in court for this sort of thing.'   (Grey Division)

A significant minority of the parents specifically mentioned the triviality of the offending behaviour involved. And if we examine closely the nature of behaviour or damages or value of goods stolen in all cases, we can find that offences of 'criminal damage' could mean breaking the window of a butcher, damaging three bags of grain in a farm or demolishing two straw stacks in the field. Similarly, the offence of 'arson' in one case involved setting fire to a waste-paper basket, whilst the value of goods stolen in theft-related offences ranged from as little as £5.50 (a toy duck), to a barrel of beer from an Indian restaurant, to £185 (a camera). Partly because of this gap between the perceived triviality of the offending behaviour and the formal charges brought by the police, parents did not always feel a caution was the best way of dealing with the incident. In one case where N (aged 12) demolished two straw-stacks in the field, the parents complained that their son would have apologized to the farmer and they would have paid compensation – 'the police should never have processed the case formally in the first place'.

(Yellow Division)

Nor did parents necessarily regard a caution as a 'let-off'. Whilst their understanding of the implications of a caution was at best vague and partial, some parents were highly sceptical of the police's claim that a caution was simply a 'private matter' between them and the juvenile:

ML: 'Do you think a caution is a let-off by the police?'
Mother: 'No, I don't. Because that could still be used against him, that isn't totally wiped out.'

(Yellow Division)

Or as other parents put it:

'It isn't really a private matter between the police and [my son]. Oh no! He's still on bail; he has done a criminal act in the eyes of the police, you know, so they can use it again, like the Inspector just said, if there's any more trouble, that can be used, that can sway what the next result would be because he's got a caution.'

(Grey Division)

'Not a let-off... because he has to be very careful from now on. The school somehow has learnt about this, and he has been very worried.'

(Grey Division)

'It's not an easy way out. He has been told off by the officer, hasn't he? For this kind of offence which is very minor really, it's a bit over-reacting if you ask me.'

(Red Division)

'It's not really a let-off. You see, there'd be a lot to do in the society if the police took everybody to court for the first offence, and probably the cost involved, and the end result of it won't be worth it.'

(Yellow Division)

DISCUSSION

For many young people who were cautioned at the police station, one thing seemed clear: they saw the purpose and administration of police cautioning in punitive terms, not in terms of offering help, guidance or encouraging parental involvement in keeping their children out of trouble. As McConville and others (1991, pp.130–1) have pointed out, both prosecution and caution are geared towards achieving similar objectives of punishment within the criminal justice process: 'in deterring further offences, in protecting the public, in bringing home to the offender the wrongfulness of the relevant conduct and in educating the offender in the social values embodied in the criminal law'. But given that most cautioning sessions last no more than 15 minutes, and without any alternative means of measuring the long term 'success' of cautioning, these objectives are collapsed into more immediate concerns of the police of achieving a visible impact on the young people on the spot (e.g. through shaming, reducing them to tears).

7 Summary and Concluding Remarks

This book has addressed the theoretical and empirical questions raised by the policing of young people and the processing of juvenile delinquents through 'informal' means outside the court system. In doing so, it has ranged across a variety of themes, viewpoints and times. The purpose of this chapter is therefore twofold: first, to summarize the key arguments raised in previous chapters; second, to tease out the various implications of my arguments.

GENERAL SUMMARY

Chapter 1 examined the use of police discretionary powers and the working through of alternative state strategies for dealing with juvenile delinquency in the historical context. Not all laws were relentlessly enforced by the police. The lingering feud-like relationship between the police and 'the policed' in some working-class neighbourhoods made it necessary for the police to turn 'half a blind eye to the rule book' and 'the other half of a blind eye to a good deal of minor infringement' (Cohen, 1979). Thus, to a large extent, the origins of police cautioning were shaped by the practical exigencies of policing. Informal police discipline, involving a stern 'telling off', moving people on, 'cuffing' or other forms of physical violence, formed part of the everyday routine for the street population. This applied particularly to the young, who had traditionally been the ready targets of police patrolling practice. The relations between the police and young people were also mediated by the enduring police service role. Involvement in juvenile welfare had long been regarded as a police duty. Backed by early quasi-sociological and psychological theories of criminogenic environment and homes, juvenile liaison strategies in the post-war years permitted the police to intervene in the lives of 'pre-delinquents' who were drifting into a criminal career or life of immorality. They involved preventive home visits, formal cautions administered by the police away from the streets and directed at the whole family and, over time, the setting up of specialized units as part of the wider bureaucratization process. Concepts of 'delinquency', 'punishment' and 'welfare treatment' were reworked not only by the police but also by the magistracy and other local state apparatus, in ways that reflected their competing claims of expert status and knowledge about the nature of social problems. The informal police processing of juvenile delinquents gathered pace since the 1960s, but the balance between the proper use of police discretion and their proper role as law enforcers was, and still is, an uneasy one. Furthermore, police service work did not wholly displace other mechanisms of the criminal justice system for dealing with the 'difficult', 'uncooperative' and 'troublesome' youths.

The next chapter reviewed the policy and the use of police caution as the predominant means of dealing with young offenders outside the formal court system in England and Wales in the contemporary context. The expansion of the use of cautioning has been associated with various strands of the diversionary movement and, from the late 1980s onwards, managerialist concerns to regulate 'inputs' into the courts because of the financial and organizational implications for the rest of the system. According to Dunkel (1991), non-prosecution is now part of a wider strategy to cope with increasing crime rates and to stabilize the case loads of criminal justice administration in many parts of Europe. One common European practice is the *conditional waiving* of prosecution whereby prosecution is withheld *provided that* some formal condition is fulfilled (e.g. reparation, or attendance at counselling sessions). But the outcome of the Conservatives' managerialist reform has been far from straightforward. First, the reform efforts are circumscribed by political discourses articulated around law and order, as the constant political necessity to clamp down on 'soft options' in crime control has led to a *destabilization* of the caseloads of the criminal justice system. Second, because the police caution decision is regarded as one rooted in the constable's common law discretion, it has remained outside statutory control. This, I argued, has important implications for the control of police decision-making. The Home Office's initiatives to oversee the cautioning system have evolved around promoting national standards for cautioning practice. In so far as inconsistent decision-making, 'unintended' consequences (for instance, 'net widening') and disparity in cautioning rates are identified as the main operational malfunctions, all that is arguably needed is a better defined focus (for instance, to define what constitutes 'diversion' and what does not), better monitoring and fine-tuning in service delivery. What this managerialist model of control fails to take into account is the use of caution and other forms of informal discipline as a multi-use resource in routine policing.

The next three chapters considered the implementation of a multi-agency approach to delinquency control, the organization of police caution decision-making, and its impact on those on the receiving-end of cautioning. In Chapter 3, I argued that the multi-agency approach has to be understood as part of a wider redefining of the *ownership* of the problem of crime in the 1990s. Just as local communities and the law-abiding citizens have been enlisted to participate in the 'war against crime', agencies and organizations from all fields have been mobilized to shoulder front-line responsibilities for preventing crime and producing public safety. But this redefining process has not gone unchallenged, and the contested ownership of the problem of juvenile delinquency is most apparent at the local level. This was the case even in the heyday of the early 1990s when multi-agency cooperation was a central plank of the official cautioning policy. Chapter 4 considered the limits and possibilities of the multi-agency consultative approach, by looking at the role of social agencies in cautioning decision-making in four localities. The key issue here relates to the police construction of 'cautionability'. However the cautioning system is organized, lower ranking police officers retain considerable power. What the front-line officers do and the type of 'cases' arresting officers push into the system, shape what the police managers and social agencies have to review and deal with. In principle, multi-agency consultation can produce 'better' and more consistent decisions by bringing to the forefront non-police values and ideologies. In reality, the expert status of the police in delinquency control remains paramount. In order to be able to influence police decisions, social agencies need to be perceived as making credible recommendations within the bounds of police priorities and practices. They must be seen as realistic and grounded in common sense, with all the connotations that carries for interpreting juvenile delinquency. In the process of gate-keeping the local court system, the task of the social agencies often becomes one of mediating client definitions of guilt or justice to administrative criteria of rationality.

Interpretations of the problem of juvenile delinquency, and assessments of what can be done about it, are also tied up with the working assumptions, histories, and diverse agendas of the key players involved in the pre-court sifting process. Chapter 5 looked at the hierarchies of knowledge among social agencies and the disputes over clients and resources that exist despite the rhetoric of multi-agency cooperation. In particular, the education welfare services are seen as the functionaries of a disreputed welfarist approach who jeopardise the work of 'real' professionals. Once again, the police are left to fill the void created by the desire of social agencies to pursue minimum intervention in young people's lives. It is no surprise that they feel they have a legitimate duty to exercise control through punishment when they believe that parents and social agencies have abdicated their responsibilities and the public are demanding it.

Chapter 6 looked at the contrasting understanding and experience of cautioning from the viewpoints of the police, young people and their parents. Police cautioning may be an 'alternative' to court, but only in a limited, i.e. administrative, sense. The staging of cautioning and the normative agenda that the police hold in assessing young people and their families remains inextricably tied up with the court-based delinquency control paradigm. The resulting contradictions are then discussed. Young people are constantly reminded of the court's authority: indeed, the scare tactics of cautioning officers routinely depend on conjuring images of the formal court system and the prison as the ultimate sanction. Parents understand, in general terms, that the police caution is about requiring them to exercise greater control over their children. Yet, parents have no control at all over the cautioning process. Many families caught up in the cautioning process clearly do not experience the twin aspects of a 'dressing down' and moral lecturing as a 'soft option'. Nor do they regard the police offer of 'help' as necessarily in their best interests.

With these issues in mind, let us consider what the future of police cautioning may hold under the New Labour government, and the implications for the policing of young people.

MORE OF THE SAME?

From the late 1980s onwards, as many critics observed (Keith and Murji, 1990; Sim and Gilroy, 1987), the left realist inspired Labour Party policies and statements on crime have become virtually indistinguishable from the Tory agenda of law and order. The New Labour's 'zero tolerance' of crime and anti-social behaviour is most apparent in its proposals for a range of stringent measures in recent years – abolition of rules that limit criminal responsibility for under-fourteens; a new 'community safety order' to restrain rowdy and noisy neighbours; action to curb public drinking, aggressive begging and intimidating activities of 'squeegee merchants'; a ban on the ownership of hand-guns and tougher penalties for weapons offences; night-time curfew on children under the age of ten (*Times*, 31 March, 1997, p.6). Successive Labour Party leaders and Shadow Home Secretaries have also denounced those in the party calling for tighter monitoring of policing as 'police bashing' and instead promised policies to bring about community support for a better resourced police service in the fight against crime. The difficulty with this approach, on a political level, is that it places the two major political parties in open competition with each other in bidding up public anxieties about crime and a more punitive response to crime control. As far as police cautioning is concerned, a new 'single final warning' has been proposed by the

Home Secretary as part of the New Labour package to ensure the emphasis in youth justice is placed first on punishment and to 'nip offending in the bud'. The proposed single warning also mirrors the previous government's 'one strike and you're out' approach to crime control – a young offender who is sent to court within two years of the warning will no longer be eligible for a conditional discharge regardless of the seriousness of the crime (*Guardian*, 21 May 1996, p.10).

Within this cross-party political agenda, there is very little space for the representation of the interests and claims of young people who are dissatisfied with the policing service that they receive. In recent years, chief police officers have tried to reorientate the culture of policing around an explicit mission of service and ethos of consumerism, partly as self-engineered change to preserve the organization but also in response to central government's reform agenda. As Reiner (1994) has pointed out, this emphasis on 'quality of service' and service delivery is arguably 'policing designed for the age of the Citizen's Charter'. Whether or not young people are regarded as 'respectable customers' for policing is debatable, however. To the extent that young people's experience of cautioning is linked with their adversarial experience of policing on the streets, police offer of help and support at the cautioning session may seem hollow. Young people as a social group have a disproportionately high level of adversary contact with the police. In Kinsey's research study (1992), over half of the total sample had experienced some form of adversary contact with the police, especially being moved on or told off and questioned about a crime by the police. This impression of unwarranted police attention is arguably exacerbated by the perception that the police do not take seriously their problems of victimization and safety. Thus, even when young people realize they have done something wrong, they often consider their actions trivial compared with the more serious things which happened to them, for which the police provide little or no protection (Anderson et al., 1994; Loader, 1996). All this can seriously limit the effectiveness of the police service role with regards to young people.

AMBIVALENCE IN CRIME MANAGEMENT

Police cautioning is essentially an alternative means of disposing of deviant bodies. The increasing dominance of technocratic rationality in case disposal decision-making is inherently unfriendly to the expert status of social work, probation and education welfare services. Whether or not some form of multi-agency partnership survives in future will depend on the ability of social agencies to facilitate the smooth functioning of this case disposal process. In such a scenario, multi-agency liaison forums can best be described as a case-processing centre for the local youth court, with managers of social agencies acting as processors for a sanctioning system that runs parallel to the formal court system.

With the rise of a market-oriented consumer approach and social auditing in the public sector, efficiency devices such as reducing court overload, delays and late guilty pleas and so on, can best be understood as part of the wider strategy of the penal system to adapt to high crime rates and high throughput. In this context, an alternative system of processing juvenile delinquents which bypasses the lengthy and costly processes of full investigation, prosecution, legal aid, and trial, may be hailed as the only way to manage the current crime problem. Pleas of guilty are no longer good enough: they must come earlier (for instance, at the police cautioning stage) rather than later. The ideal-type of an efficient criminal justice system, according to Carol Jones (1993), would appear to be one which engages in administration rather than adjudication. It would be a 'trial free' system, in which fewer people would use the formal processes of law.

As political pressure builds to find credible penal strategies to keep low-risk offenders in the community, police cautioning will most certainly continue to occupy centre stage in crime management. But a number of ambiguities remain. In much 'common-sense' discussion and in popular press imagery, penalties which are not court-based are not regarded as 'proper' punishments at all. The equation between punishment and court sanctions for many people (including front-line officers) is so strong that for the offender to be given a chastisement by the police is for them to be a 'let-off'. The consequence is that in recent years we have witnessed a remarkably ambivalent pattern of policy development. On the one hand, there has been an attempt on the part of the state to normalize crime and develop new pragmatic strategies to replace the idea of winning a 'war against crime'. Even official discourse on crime control now suggests that 'criminality is not confined to a small minority, but is evident at some time in the lives of many' (Audit Commission, 1993, p.6). But these pragmatic adaptations to the uncomfortable reality of high crime rates have coexisted with quite contradictory discourses in respect of the crime problem. Thus, concerted attempts to reduce the costs of crime control expenditure and 'define deviance down' (Garland, 1996) are often undercut by punitive pronouncements on the part of government ministers that throw the whole process into chaos. One can perhaps argue that the 'law and order' paradigm is too deeply inscribed, and too politically potent, to be easily dismantled by managerialist critique and administrative reform, and we will continue to observe its invocation under New Labour administration. Against this background, police cautioning stands at the intersection of a variety of interests and competing demands, and will continue to generate new sites of negotiation and alliance as well as social conflict.

Appendix

The empirical research on which this book is based took place between 1990 and 1992 in four police force divisions in south-east England. Between 1990 and 1992 I observed 73 multi-agency liaison meetings and conducted a series of semi-structured interviews with a total of 155 practitioners, juveniles and their parents. A great deal of detailed, qualitative material was obtained during the research contact outlined above, and full transcripts were made of all interviews. These, running to nearly a thousand pages, were read and reread innumerable times in order that the reiterated themes, continuities and contradictions could be taken up to structure and inform, first, the ethnographic analyses of the professional activities and discourses of those charged with diverting juveniles from court (Chapters 3, 4 and 5); and, second, the experiences and perspectives of those at the receiving-end of cautioning (Chapter 6).

Table A.1 Number of multi-agency meetings observed and cases studied

	Meetings observed	*Cases studied*
Red Division	21	132
Yellow Division	20	68
Grey Division	18	120
Blue Division	14	82

Table A.2 Number of people interviewed

Category	*Number of people interviewed*
Probation Service	4
Social services	10
Education welfare	7
Youth & Community	1
Police	34
Magistrates	14
Juveniles (male)	31
Juveniles (female)	4
Parents	48
Care worker	2

Notes

INTRODUCTION

1. In a similar case, a West Yorkshire community constable was convicted and fined for assaulting a 15-year-old boy as the officer 'attempted to stop his rowdy behaviour in a shopping arcade' (*Guardian*, 20 December 1995).
2. Source: GMTV Press Office, 1995; quoted in McKenzie (1995), p. 195.
3. *Police Review*, 22 July 1994, p. 9; 29 July 1994, p. 6.
4. Prime Minister John Major, speech at Church House, London, 9 September 1994; quoted in *NACRO Criminal Justice Digest*, October 1994, p. 26.
5. *The Independent*, 15 June 1994. The Metropolitan Police Commissioner Sir Paul Condon's controversial comments about 'noble cause corruption' almost a year after the Guscott case also struck a chord with many officers who have long complained there are too many rules stacked against them (*Police Review*, 24 March 1995, p. 14; 14 July 1995, p. 16).

1 THE POLICING OF JUVENILE DELINQUENCY

1. The police of Paris, for example, supervised lost and abandoned children. Distraught parents from poorer sections of society were even known to ask the Lieutenant of Police to lock up their uncontrollable children (Emsley, 1983).
2. In practice, the regimes for 'care and protection' were harsh: early industrial schools replicated the brutality and long working hours of industrial employment and maintained the practice of public birching and caning, solitary confinement, and bread-and-water diet as punishment for boys, and corporal punishment, spanking, extra bedmaking, scrubbing, and the deprivation of 'privileges' for girls (Barnett, 1913).
3. Vagrancy and idleness, especially among the young, were faults which penal reformers perceived as rampant in sections of the working class and a precursor to hardened criminality. The penitentiary was developed at roughly the same time as the workhouse under the New Poor Law; the parallel with the control system of the new factory can also be drawn (see Emsley, 1987; Ignatieff, 1978).

139

4. Gatrell (1980) suggested that the Education Act of 1870 and its compulsory clause probably did more than reformatories and the like to remove juveniles from the street and keep them from crime.
5. The discipline in these reformatory schools was generally harsh: some even introduced the barred windows, locked doors, and cropped hair which continued to be a feature of their regimes until the 1920s (*First Report on the Work of the Children's Branch*, 1923). Reformation was essentially based on middle-class construction of social hierarchies and deference. For instance, inculcation of regular work habits through performance of semi-skilled and unskilled labouring tasks – including brick-making, wood-chopping and paper salvage for boys, and laundry work for girls – formed the main basis for 'discipline through labour' (*22nd Report of the Inspector of Reformatory and Industrial Schools*, 1879).
6. *Report to the Secretary of State for the Home Department on the State of the Law Relating to the Treatment and Punishment of Juvenile Offenders*, 1881, p. 49.
7. With the publication of crime statistics after 1805, many were convinced that crime was increasing. Committals to trial, for instance, went up by four and a half times between 1805 and 1842 (Smith, 1985). However, some historians argued this could reflect a hardening of attitudes to crime, policy decisions to crack down on particular offences, or a greater willingness to prosecute, and not necessarily a large increase in crime. For a discussion of the problems inherent in interpreting criminal statistics, see Emsley, 1983; Beattie, 1974; Gatrell, 1980; Tobias, 1967; Maguire, 1994.
8. Quoted in Schaffer (1980), p. 29.
9. Under another juvenile liaison scheme in West Ham, police supervision, designed to be 'not intensive' but 'frequent enough to keep an eye on a child', involved introducing the juveniles into youth clubs, arranging holidays and discouraging them from mixing with other delinquents (Taylor, 1971, p. 42). Those parents who were considered to be ineffective also received guidance on their child's upbringing – for instance, 'to give less pocket money or to make fewer demands of the child if he was exceptionally dull' (ibid, p. 21).
10. Maureen Cain (1968) found that when the role conflict became too great for some police juvenile liaison officers in the forces she studied, they left in order to become probation officers.
11. Similarly, the introduction of private hearings under the 1933 Children and Young Persons Act and successive efforts to simplify the legal procedures were arguably geared not only towards mitigating the stigma attached to a juvenile court appearance, but also towards overcoming the reluctance of the police, the education authorities, social workers and the general public to bring delinquents before the courts (Bailey, 1987).

12. In his examination of the struggles for the direction of delinquency control policy within and around the Children's Branch between 1913 and 1930, Clarke (1982, pp. 29–33) argued that the emergent ideology of scientific knowledge and expert professionalism reflected a political struggle to transform the basis of state intervention in delinquency 'from moral, religious and political criteria' embodied in the voluntary and charitable sector (for instance, the old reformatory and industrial schools, the missionary probation officers) to 'universal scientific and technical ones', enforced by 'a body of state functionaries' under centralized direction.

13. *Justice of the Peace and Local Government Review*, 1 September 1928, Vol.XCIL, p. 570.

14. *Justice of the Peace and Local Government Review*, 20 October 1928, p. 678.

15. *The Justice of the Peace*, 13 January 1923, Vol. LXXXVII, p. 27.

16. 'War and Probation', *Justice of the Peace and Local Government Review*, 27 January 1940, p. 44.

17. 'Admonition of Juveniles', *Justice of the Peace and Local Government Review*, 29 April 1944, p. 205.

18. 'Juvenile Admonition Panels', *Justice of the Peace and Local Government Review*, 22 April 1944, p. 200.

19. 'Admonition of Juveniles', *Justice of the Peace and Local Government Review*, 29 April 1944, p. 205.

20. 'Police Cautions for Juveniles', *Justice of the Peace and Local Government Review*, 11 August 1945, p. 375.

21. *The Magistrate*, 1943, Vol.6, pp. 206–7.

22. 'Juvenile Admonition Panels', *Justice of the Peace and Local Government Review*, 22 April 1944, p. 200.

23. In Scotland legislative provision affecting juvenile offenders up to the 1960s broadly paralleled that in England and Wales. The Kilbrandon Committee (1964), set up to look into the provisions of law and the juvenile courts in Scotland, upheld the concept of individualized treatment but went further than its counterparts in England and Wales in proposing diverting juveniles from formal court proceedings and abolishing the juvenile court system. Whereas the proposed family councils were venomously attacked in England around the same time, objections to the reform proposals in Scotland were 'extraordinarily muted' (Bottoms, 1974; Morris, 1974). The juvenile court was eventually abolished under the Social Work (Scotland) Act 1968 and replaced by a form of proceedings known as the Children's Hearings (Morris and McIsaac, 1978; Martin et al., 1981; Kelly, 1996). The proceedings are based on the admission of the offence or acceptance of the ground of referral by the child and the parents. If the child or the parent denies the ground of referral (for instance, the commission of the

offence) the case is referred to the sheriff court for the offence to be proved or dismissed.

24. Whether or not there is a valid role for the police in moral education is debatable, especially when the targeted children are often the youngest age-groups and are least likely to challenge police conceptions of law, order, and citizenship. Whilst police presence in schools was a central part of community policing initiatives in the 1970s and 1980s, it was viewed as being sensitive precisely because there were doubts about the propriety of using the police for such a function (Gordon, 1987; Carter and Coussins, 1991; Menter, 1987).

2 CONTROLLING CAUTIONING PRACTICE AND POLICE DISCRETION

1. Similarly, in the United States, 'diversion', as a juvenile justice programme alternative in the late 1960s, became popular as a result of concerns about the overreach of the justice system into the lives of minor and 'status' offenders and the perceived failure of traditional programmes to resolve the problem of juvenile delinquency (President's Commission on Law Enforcement and Administration of Justice, 1967; see also Sarri, 1983; Klein, 1979; Lemert, 1971, 1981).
2. The Parliamentary All-Party Penal Affairs Group's Report (1981) on young offenders also gave strong support to the use of formal caution for all first and second minor offenders under seventeen as a form of 'diversion from the criminal justice system'.
3. Up until 1985 the police had the unique right to initiate and conduct prosecutions, mainly through their own prosecuting departments headed by senior police officers and staffed by civilian solicitors. With the establishment of the CPS, the crown prosecutors have responsibility for the conduct of the case in court, may drop or amend charges and, in theory, have ultimate veto of prosecution. The prosecutorial discretion of the CPS is in turn subject to judicial review, as a growing body of case law covers decisions not to prosecute as well as decisions to prosecute (e.g. in *R.* v. *Chief Constable of the Kent County Constabulary, ex p. L*) (Hilson, 1993).
4. Apart from these formal preconditions, other factors considered relevant to caution decisions include the offender's previous record and attitude to the offence. References to the offender's character and family circumstances, which appeared in the 1985 Home Office cautioning circular, were omitted from the 1990 and 1994 cautioning circulars.
5. *Guardian*, 22 February 1993, p. 2.

6. Research into the criminal histories of those cautioned indicates an apparently high 'success' rate: 82 per cent of all offenders (adult and juvenile) cautioned in 1991 were not convicted for a 'standard list' offence within two years of the caution (Home Office, 1994b).
7. See, for instance, *Police Review*, 26 February 1993, p. 3; 5 March 1993, pp. 16–17; 20 August 1993, pp. 24–5.
8. Ashworth and Fionda (1994, p. 899) argued that even the principle of restraint in dealing with young offenders has now been de-emphasized in the 1994 revised *Code for Crown Prosecutors*:

> The general principle that the prosecution of young defendants should be a last resort has disappeared entirely. Paragraph 21 of the former Code stated that a caution should be considered as an alternative to prosecution, and that juveniles should not be prosecuted unless 'exceptional circumstances dictate otherwise'. None of this survives into the new Code, which rather reflects the cold blow of the Home Secretary's changed policies.

Whether the 1994 *Code for Crown Prosecutors* represents a clear shift of policy or 'mere clarification of existing practice' has been a subject for debate (see Daw, 1994).
9. Home Secretary Michael Howard at the press conference held to launch the 1994 cautioning circular. Reported in the *Guardian* and *The Times*, 16 March 1994.
10. Early research studies also highlighted variations in cautioning rates between police forces that were too great to be explained in terms of differences in types of crime or juvenile delinquency rates in the different local areas (Patchett and McClean, 1965; Sebba, 1967; McClintock and Avison, 1968; Somerville, 1969; Steer, 1970; Rainton, 1974).
11. For a useful review, see Reiner (1985) and Brogden et al. (1988).
12. Other research studies have documented the disproportionate use of stop and search powers (Willis, 1983; Walker et al., 1989), the state of police–black relations in the inner cities (Humphry and John, 1972), and black people's experience of police racism in the streets and at police stations (NACRO, 1991). The Policy Studies Institute suggested that the police tended to hold stereotypical notions of West Indian families as being 'disorganized' and 'criminogenic', hence affecting their decisions whether or not to caution. Moreover, to the extent that black juveniles were regarded as a worse risk (or 'undeserving' offenders) because of a perceived disrespectful 'stroppiness', or if they or their parents appeared less willing to accept a caution, this would also adversely affect their cautioning rate (Smith and Gray, 1983).

13. It is also problematic to treat racism in the policing of juveniles as an all-pervasive, monolithic phenomenon. The police may hold different stereotypical attitudes towards different minority ethnic groups. Young West Indians were seen as the most difficult group by the police, whereas Asians were often perceived as 'no great problem, but liars if suspected of wrong doing' (quoted in Brogden et al.,1988, p. 126). As far as attitudes to the police are concerned, Asians seemed to be less critical than West Indians, though more so than whites (Smith and Gray, 1983).

14. This, however, raises the problem that females who do not fit into gender stereotypes, i.e. those who do not confess their wrongdoing, express their remorse in particular ways, or even commit 'typical' crimes such as shoplifting, may be seen as doubly pathological and treated more harshly.

15. Instead of diverting juvenile delinquents from custody, only one in six or eight of the estimated 25 000 young people placed under IT in 1979 were subject to any formal court order (National Youth Bureau, 1979).

16. An alternative test of the net-widening thesis has concentrated on the total volume of cautions and prosecutions. It was acknowledged that, in the 1970s, the growth in police cautioning in England and Wales was not accompanied by an immediate direct reduction in the overall number of juveniles who were dealt with in court (Morris, 1978). By the late 1980s, however, there was a significant reduction in both the total volume of cautions and prosecutions. This has led critics to argue that 'net-widening', at least in the statistical sense, may not be a continuing feature of current penal practice.

17. Whilst the 1994 Home Office cautioning circular makes no clear recommendations regarding Caution Plus, the Audit Commission's (1996) report is in favour of greater use of schemes that work with families to target early offenders.

18. Whether the 'institutional reparative model' whereby a youth is required to apologize to a representative of some organization offers scope for reconciliation is debatable (Blagg, 1985). Store managers may be regarded by the young people as just another authority figure (security guards, police officers, teachers and so on) delivering a moral lecture. Furthermore, reparation may be perceived as a 'shaming' session by the offender, or indeed intended to be one by the authorities.

3 MANAGING YOUTH CRIME THROUGH MULTI-AGENCY PARTNERSHIPS

1. In a subsequent article, the chief officers from the five parent agencies (O'Dowd et al., 1991) defended the work of their JLB in North-

ampton and argued that some of the latest developments – for instance, the Bureau's work in reparation, mediation, offence resolution and offender support – represented a positive approach to juvenile offending.

2. Although high cautioning rates were supported by senior police officers in Northamptonshire, Hughes et al. (1995, p. 5) found that misgivings were evident amongst the junior officers:

> Such measures of 'success' may of course be reinterpreted as measures of failure as appeared to be the case among elements of the police where the rank and file 'canteen culture', on occasions, jokingly called the JLBs 'Juvenile Let-off Bureaux'.

3. In 1990 a total of 1170 juvenile offence cases were recorded by the Red Division police.

4. To the police, maintaining order in and around the City Football Ground was considered a top policing priority. The result was a strong presumption to prosecute all offences committed in football grounds – i.e. what Sanders (1985b) has termed 'policy prosecution' – rather than bringing those cases before the JJB for joint decision-making.

5. A total of 320 cases were brought before the JJB for discussion in 1990. Of the completed cases just under half resulted in a decision to caution, 40 per cent in a decision to prosecute, and the rest in a decision of 'no further action'.

6. In 1990, a total of 169 cases were brought before the JLB in Yellow Division for discussion, of which 35 per cent resulted in a decision to prosecute, 61 per cent in a decision to caution, and 4 per cent in a decision of 'no further action'.

7. In 1990, about 560 juvenile offence cases were dealt with by the police in Grey Division. Of these, 8 per cent was directly charged by the police without referral to the Liaison Panel; another 21 per cent was given an 'instant caution', an informal warning or 'no further action'. Just over 400 cases were brought to the attention of the Liaison Panel, of which a decision to prosecute was recorded against 30 per cent of the cases.

8. In 1990, just over 670 juvenile offence cases were dealt with by the police in Blue Division. Of these, about 10 per cent were directly charged by the police, another 27 per cent were given an 'instant caution', informal warning or 'no further action'. About 280 were then brought to the attention of the Liaison Panel, of which a decision to prosecute was recorded against 55 per cent of the cases.

9. In Red Division, for instance, the number of juveniles found guilty of indictable offences in court was reduced from 230 in 1982 to just over 100 in 1990. Similarly, in Yellow Division, the number of

juveniles found guilty of indictable offences in court was reduced from 120 in 1982 to 55 in 1990.

10. A less cynical interpretation of the change is that the youth court's jurisdiction is in line with the United Nations Standard Minimum Rules for the Administration of Juvenile Justice and the United Nations Convention on the Rights of the Child. These provide that a child, i.e. a person under eighteen years of age, should be dealt with under a separate jurisdiction and subject to a range of penalties and dispositions that take into account his or her welfare (Gelsthorpe and Morris, 1994).

4   CONSTRUCTING THE CASE FOR CAUTION

1. The 1982 Criminal Act, for instance, introduced the controversial night restriction orders in order to reinforce parental authority in the control of adolescent family members. Critics, however, argued that since young people who appear before the courts often come from troubled families, they are unlikely to be assisted by extending the time spent compulsorily in one another's company.

5   CONFLICTS IN MULTI-AGENCY LIAISON

1. In 1981, 11 840 juveniles were made subject to a supervision order (including supervision under the CYPA 1969 following care proceedings) and supervised by the probation service. By 1991 the number had reduced to 2307. In 1981, 47 480 social inquiry reports were prepared by probation officers for the juvenile court. By 1991 the number had fallen to 7835 (Home Office, 1993).
2. Not all probation services withdrew from working with juvenile offenders. In some areas, no agreement was reached with social services and the probation service retained responsibility for a significant number of juvenile offenders. In other areas, the service had developed joint work with their local social services department, e.g. inter-agency juvenile justice units (HM Inspectorate of Probation, 1994).
3. In an article in *The Magistrate* (June 1991), John Harding from the Association of Chief Officers of Probation Service reaffirmed the notion of inter-agency planning but, in another context, suggested that probation should adopt a leading role in the youth court. This led to a sharp rebuke from Charles Bell (1991) from the Association of Juvenile Justice, who argued that social services departments should take a 'primary or sole responsibility' in respect of pre-sentence reports and the supervision of sixteen- and seventeen-year-olds.

6 RECEIVING POLICE CAUTIONING

1. Similarly, Parker et al. (1981, p. 100) suggested that a significant number of females in their sample received similar reassurances from the police, and were often left with feelings of anger and resentment when they were eventually charged and summoned to court.

2. In response, the police may use various means to get round the legal constraints – 'informal' interrogations in the absence of an appropriate adult to secure information about other unsolved crimes, 'rule bending' by playing on the fears of the parents and juveniles or through the use of 'ploys' (Sanders and Bridges, 1990).

3. Similarly, research commissioned by the 1993 Royal Commission on Criminal Justice found that 'the presence of legal advisers in interrogations is often seen as an unwarranted invasion of the citadel of investigative policing' (McConville and Hodgson, 1993, p. 155). This was despite the passive role they actually played and their reluctance to intervene even in the face of overly harsh interrogation strategies or where the questions were improper, inappropriate and irrelevant.

4. In drug enforcement, police pressure on the offender to pass on intelligence can translate as the practice of taking a potentially more 'lenient' approach to the disposal of drug possession offenders who give information about their dealer, or of drug traffickers who give information about more 'weighty' traffickers. And for some offenders, the original inducement of a caution marks the beginning of a 'career' as a police informant (Dorn and Murji, 1992; Dorn, 1994).

Bibliography

Adams, R., Allard, S., Baldwin, J. and Thomas, J. (1981) *A Measure of Diversion* (Leicester: National Youth Bureau).

Advisory Council on the Misuse of Drugs (ACMD) (1994) *Drug Misusers and the Criminal Justice System, Part II: Police, Drug Misusers and the Community* (London: HMSO).

Ainsworth, P. and Pease, K. (1987) *Police Work* (London: British Psychological Society and Methuen).

Alderson, J. (1980) *Policing Freedom* (Plymouth: MacDonald & Evans).

Allen, H. (1987) *Justice Unbalanced* (Milton Keynes: Open University Press).

Allen, R. (1991b) 'Parental Responsibility for Juvenile Offenders', in T. Booth (ed.), *Juvenile Justice in the New Europe* (Sheffield: Joint Unit for Social Services Research).

Anderson, S., Kinsey, R., Loader, I. and Smith, C. (1994) *Cautionary Tales. Young people, Crime and Policing in Edinburgh* (Aldershot: Avebury).

Ashworth, A. (1989) *Custody Reconsidered: clarity and consistency in sentencing* (London: Centre for Policy Studies).

Ashworth, A. and Fionda, J. (1994) 'The New Code for Crown Prosecutors: Prosecution, Accountability and the Public Interest', *Criminal Law Review*, December 1994, pp. 894–903.

Association of Chief Police Officers (ACPO) (1989) *The Diversion of Juveniles from the Formal Criminal Justice System* (London: ACPO).

Association of Chief Police Officers (ACPO) (1990) *Setting the Standards: Meeting Community Expectation* (London: ACPO).

Association of Chief Police Officers (ACPO) (1995) *The Cautioning of Offenders* (London: ACPO).

Audit Commission (1993) *Helping with Enquiries: Tackling Crime Effectively* (London: HMSO).

Audit Commission (1996) *Misspent Youth: Young People and Crime* (London: HMSO).

Austin, J. and Krisberg, B. (1981) 'Wider, Stronger, Different Nets: The Dialectics of Criminal Justice Reform', *Journal of Research in Crime and Delinquency*, vol. 18(1), pp. 165–96.

Bailey, V. (1981) (ed.) *Policing and Punishment in the Nineteenth Century* (London: Croom Helm).

Bailey, V. (1987) *Delinquency and Citizenship* (Oxford: Clarendon Press).

Baldwin, J. and McConville, M. (1977) *Negotiated Justice* (London: Martin Robertson).

Banton, M. (1964) *The Policeman in the Community* (London: Tavistock).

Barnett, M. (1913) *Young Delinquents* (London: Methuen).

Bayley, D.H. (1977) (ed.) *Police and Society* (London: Sage).

Becker, H. (1963) *Outsiders: Studies in the Sociology of Deviance* (New York: Free Press of Glencoe).

Becker, H. (1967) *The Other Side: Perspectives on Deviance* (London: Collier-Macmillan).

Bell, C. (1991) 'Future Arrangements for Servicing the Youth Court – a Challenge to the Proposed Way Forward', *Justice of the Peace*, October 1991, pp. 686–9.

Bell, C. and Haines, K. (1991) 'Managing the Transition: Implications of the Introduction of a Youth Court in England and Wales', in T. Booth (ed.), *Juvenile Justice in the New Europe* (Sheffield: Joint Unit for Social Services Research).

Bennett, T. (1979) 'The Social Distribution of Criminal Labels', *British Journal of Criminology*, vol. 19(2), pp. 134–45.

Blackwell, G. (1990) 'In on the Act', *Community Care*, 10 May, pp. 13–15.

Blagg, H. (1985) 'Reparation and Justice for Juveniles', *British Journal of Criminology*, vol. 25(4), pp. 267–79.

Blagg, H. et al. (1986) *The Final Report on the Juvenile Liaison Bureau, Corby*. University of Lancaster, unpublished.

Blagg, H., Pearson, G., Sampson, A., Smith, D. and Stubbs, P. (1988) 'Inter-agency co-ordination: rhetoric and reality', in T. Hope and M. Shaw (eds), *Communities and Crime Reduction* (London: HMSO).

Blagg, H. and Smith, D. (1989) *Crime, Penal Policy and Social Work* (London: Longman).

Block, B. (1989), 'Juvenile Diversion: From Court or From Justice?', *Justice of the Peace*, 9 September, pp. 574–7.

Booth, T. (1991) (ed.) *Juvenile Justice in the New Europe*. Social Services Monographs: Research in Practice. (Sheffield: Joint Unit for Social Services Research).

Bottoms, A. (1974) 'On the Decriminalisation of the English Juvenile Court', in R. Hood (ed.), *Crime, Criminology and Public Policy* (London: Heinemann).

Bottoms, A. (1977) 'Reflections on the Renaissance of Dangerousness', *Howard Journal*, vol. 16, pp. 70–96.

Bottoms, A. and McClean, J. (1976) *Defendants in the Criminal Process* (London: Routledge).

Bottoms, A. et al. (1990) *Intermediate Treatment and Juvenile Justice: Key Findings and Implications from a National Survey of Intermediate Treatment Policy and Practice* (London: HMSO).

Bowden, J. and Stevens, M. (1986) 'Justice for Juveniles – a Corporate Strategy in Northampton', *Justice of the Peace*, May 1986, pp. 326–9; pp. 345–7.

Brogden, M. (1982) *The Police: Autonomy and Consent* (London: Academic Press).

Brogden, M., Jefferson, T., Walklate, S. (1988) *Introducing Policework* (London: Unwin Hyman).

Brogden, M. (1991) *On the Mersey Beat* (Oxford: Oxford University Press).

Brown, S. (1991) *Magistrates at Work* (Milton Keynes: Open University Press).

Burt, C. (1925) *The Young Delinquent* (London: University of London Press).

Cain, M. (1968) 'Role conflict among police juvenile liaison officers', *British Journal of Criminology*, vol. 8(3), pp. 366–82.

Cain, M. (1973) *Society and the Policeman's Role* (London: Routledge & Kegan Paul).

Cain, M. and Dearden, M. (1966) 'Initial Reactions to a New Juvenile Liaison Scheme', *British Journal of Criminology*, vol. 6(4), pp. 421–30.

Carlen, P., Gleeson, D. and Wardhaugh, J. (1992) *Truancy – the Politics of Compulsory Schooling* (Buckingham: Open University Press).

Carpenter, M. (1851) *Reformatory Schools for the Children of the Perishing and Dangerous Classes and for Juvenile Offenders* (London: Gilpin).

Carter, T. and Coussins, J. (1991) 'Back to School? The Police, the education system and the black community', in E. Cashmore and E. McLaughlin (eds), *Out of Order? Policing Black People* (London: Routledge).

Cashmore, E. and McLaughlin, E. (1991) 'Out of Order?', in E. Cashmore and E. McLaughlin (eds), *Out of Order? Policing Black People* (London: Routledge).

Centre of Youth, Crime and Community (1984) *Diversion: Corporate Action with Juveniles* (Lancaster: University of Lancaster).

Children and Young Persons Review Group in Northern Ireland (1979) *Legislation and Services for Children and Young Persons in Northern Ireland (The Black Committee Report)* (Belfast: HMSO).

Christie, N. (1986) 'The Ideal Victim', in E. Fattah (ed.), *From Crime Policy to Victim Policy* (London: Macmillan).

Clarke, J., Langan, M. and Lee, P. (1980) 'Social work: the conditions of crisis', in P. Carlen and M. Collison (eds), *Radical Issues in Criminology* (New Jersey: Barnes & Noble).

Clarke, J. (1980) 'Social democratic delinquents and Fabian families', in National Deviancy Conference (ed.), *Permissiveness and Control* (London: Macmillan).

Clarke, J. (1982) *Managing the Delinquent: the Children's Branch of the Home office 1913–1930* (Milton Keynes: Open University).

Clarke, J. (1985) 'Whose Justice? The Politics of Juvenile Control', *International Journal of the Sociology of Law*, vol. 13, pp. 407–21.

Cohen, P. (1979) 'Policing the working-class city', in B. Fine et al. (eds), *Capitalism and the Rule of Law* (London: Hutchinson).

Cohen, S. (1973) *Folk devils and moral panics: the creation of mods and rockers* (St Albans: Paladin).

Cohen, S. (1985) *Visions of Social Control* (Cambridge: Polity Press).

Cooper, J. (1970) 'Social Care and Social Control', *Probation*, vol. 16, pp. 22–5.

Collison, M. (1980) 'Questions of juvenile justice', in P. Carlen and M. Collison (eds), *Radical Issues in Criminology* (New Jersey: Barnes & Noble).

Collison, M. (1995) *Police, Drugs and Community* (London: Free Association Books).

Crawford, A. (1994) 'The Partnership Approach to Community Crime Prevention: Corporatism at the Local Level?', *Social and Legal Studies*, vol. 3(4), pp. 497–519.

Crown Prosecution Service (1986) *Code for Crown Prosecutors* (London: HMSO).

Crown Prosecution Service (1990) *Code for Crown Prosecutors* (London: HMSO).

Davis, G., Boucherat, J., Watson, D. (1989) 'Pre-court decision-making in juvenile justice', *British Journal of Criminology*, vol. 29 (3), pp. 219–35.

Davis, J.S. (1989a) 'Prosecutions and their context: the use of the criminal law in later nineteenth-century London' in D. Hay and F. Snyder (eds), *Policing and Prosecution in Britain 1750–1850* (Oxford: Clarendon Press).

Davis, J.S. (1989b) 'Jennings' Building and the Royal Borough – The construction of the underclass in mid-Victorian England' in D. Feldman and G.S. Jones (eds), *London Metropolis – Histories and representations since 1800* (London: Routledge).

Daw, R. (1994) 'A Response', *Criminal Law Review*, December 1994, pp. 904–9.

Departmental Committee on the Treatment of Young Offenders (1925–6) *Minutes of Evidence*.

Department of Health and Social Security (1983) *Further Developments of Intermediate Treatment*, L.A.C. 83/3, W.O.C. 48/83.

Ditchfield, J. (1976) *Police Cautioning in England and Wales*, Home Office Research Study No. 37 (London: HMSO).

Donzelot, J. (1980) *The Policing of Families* (London: Hutchinson).

Dorn, N. (1994) 'Three Faces of Police Referral: welfare, Justice and Business Perspectives on Multi-Agency Work with Drug Arrestees', *Policing and Society*, vol. 4, pp. 13–34.

Dorn, N. and Murji, K. (1992) 'What is low level drug enforcement?' Unpublished Working Paper on the low level drug enforcement research project (London: Institute for the Study of Drug Dependence).

Dunkel, F. (1991) 'Legal Differences in Juvenile Criminology in Europe', in T. Booth (ed.), *Juvenile Justice in the New Europe* (Sheffield: Joint Unit for Social Services Research).

Edwards, S. (1984) *Women On Trial* (Manchester: University Press).

Edwards, S. (1992) 'Parental responsibility: an instrument of social policy', *Family Law*, 22, pp. 113–18.

Elliott, D. (1988) *Gender, Delinquency and Society: a Comparative Study of Male and Female Offenders and Juvenile Justice in Britain* (Aldershot: Avebury).

Emsley, C. (1983) *Policing and its Context 1750–1870* (London: Macmillan).

Emsley, C. (1987) *Crime and Society in England 1750–1900* (London: Longman).

Emsley, C. (1991) *The English Police. A Political and Social History* (Hemel Hempstead: Harvester Wheatsheaf).

Evans, R. (1991) 'Police Cautioning and the Young Adult Offender', *Criminal Law Review*, August 1991, pp. 598–609.

Evans, R. (1992) *Evaluating and Comparing Young Adult Diversion Schemes in the Metropolitan Police Area*. Report to the Home Office Research and Planning Unit.

Evans, R. (1993a) 'Evaluating Young Adult Diversion Schemes in the Metropolitan Police District', *Criminal Law Review*, July 1993, pp. 490–7.

Evans, R. (1993b) 'Comparing Young Adult and Juvenile Cautioning in the Metropolitan Police District', *Criminal Law Review*, August 1993, pp. 572–8.

Evans, R. (1993c) 'Before the Court – Understanding Inter-Agency Consultation with Juveniles and Young Adults'. Paper given at the 1993 British Criminology Conference, University of Wales, Cardiff.

Evans, R. (1993d) *The Conduct of Police Interviews with Juveniles*. Royal Commission Research Studies No.8 (London: HMSO).

Evans, R. and Ferguson, T. (1991) *Comparing Different Juvenile Cautioning Systems in One Police Force Area*. Report to the Home Office Research and Planning Unit.

Evans, R. and Wilkinson, C. (1988) *The Impact of Home Office Circular 14/1985 on Police Cautioning Policy and Practice in England and Wales*. Report to the Home Office Research and Planning Unit.

Evans, R. and Wilkinson, C. (1990) *Young Adult Offenders in Northamptonshire*. Report to the Home Office Research and Planning Unit.

Evans, R. (1994) 'Cautioning: Counting the Cost of Retrenchment', *Criminal Law Review*, August 1994, pp. 566–75.

Evans, R. (1996) 'Challenging a Police Caution Using Judicial Review', *Criminal Law Review*, February 1996, pp. 104–8.

Farrington, D., and Bennett, T. (1981) 'Police Cautioning of Juveniles in London', *British Journal of Criminology*, vol. 21(2), pp. 123–35.

Feeley, S. and Simon, J. (1992) 'The new penology: notes on the emerging strategy of corrections and its implications', *Criminology*, vol. 30(4), pp. 452–74.

Fine, B., Kinsey, R., Lea, J., Picciotto, S. and Young, J. (eds) (1979) *Capitalism and the Rule of Law* (London: Hutchinson).

Finlayson, A. (1989) 'An Alternative System of Juvenile Justice – the Scottish System', in A. Manchester and A. Giles, (eds), *Juvenile Offenders and Juvenile Justice* (British Juvenile and Family Courts Society).

Fisher, C. and Mawby, R. (1982) 'Juvenile delinquency and police discretion in an inner city area', *British Journal of Criminology*, vol. 22(1), pp. 63–75.

Forrester, M., Chatterton, M., and Pease, K. (1988) *The Kirholt Burglary Prevention Project* (London: HMSO).

Foucault, M. (1977) *Discipline and Punish* (Harmondsworth: Penguin).

Friend, J. et al. (1981) *Alcohol-related Problems: a Study of Inter-organizational Relations*. Report to SSRC (London: Tavistock Institute of Human Relations).

Garfinkel, H. (1956) 'Conditions of successful degradation ceremonies', *American Journal of Sociology*, pp. 420–4.

Garland, D. (1985) *Punishment and Welfare* (Aldershot: Gower).

Garland, D. (1990) *Punishment and Society* (Oxford: Clarendon).

Garland, D. (1996) 'The Limits of the Sovereign State – Strategies of Crime Control in Contemporary Society', *British Journal of Criminology*, 36(4), pp. 445–71.

Garton, A. (1980) 'Mutual Perceptions between Police and Probation Officers: a Research Note', *British Journal of Social Work*, vol. 10, pp. 87–9.

Gatrell, V. (1980) 'The Decline of Theft and Violence in Victorian and Edwardian England', in Gatrell, V., Lenman, B. and Parker, G. (eds), *Crime and Law: the Social History of Crime in Western Europe since 1500* (London: Europa).

Gatrell, V., Lenman, B., and Parker, G. (1980) (eds), *Crime and the Law: the Social History of Crime in Western Europe Since 1500* (London: Europa).

Geach, H. and Szwed, E. (1983) *Providing Civil Justice for Children* (London: Edward Arnold).

Gelsthorpe, L. (1989a) *Sexism and the Female Offender* (Aldershot: Gower).

Gelsthorpe, L. and Giller, H. (1990) 'More Justice for Juveniles: Does More Mean Better?', *Criminal Law Review*, March 1990, pp. 153–64.

Gelsthorpe, L. and Morris, A. (1994) 'Juvenile Justice 1945–1992', M. Maguire et al. (eds), *The Oxford Handbook of Criminology* (Oxford: Clarendon Press).

Giller, H. and Covington, C. (1983) 'Structuring discretion: question or answer?' in H.Giller and A.Morris (eds), *Providing Criminal Justice for Children* (London: Edward Arnold).

Giller, H. and Morris, A. (1977) 'The Juvenile Court – the Clients' Perspective', *Criminal Law Review*, April 1977, pp. 198–205.

Giller, H. and Morris, A. (1981) *Care and Discretion: Social Workers' Decisions with Delinquents* (London: Burnett Books).

Giller, H. and Tutt, N. (1987) 'Police Cautioning of Juveniles: the Continuing Practice of Diversity', *Criminal Law Review*, 1987, pp. 367–74.

Gillis, J. (1975) 'The evolution of juvenile delinquency in England 1890–1914', *Past and Present*, no.67, pp. 96–126.

Gordon, P. (1987) 'Community Policing: Towards the Local Police State?' in Scraton, P. (ed.), *Law, Order and the Authoritarian State* (Milton Keynes: Open University Press).

Grimshaw, R. and Jefferson, T. (1987) *Interpreting Policework* (London: Allen & Unwin).

Hall, S., Critcher, C., Jefferson, T., Clarke, J., Roberts, B. (1978) *Policing the Crisis* (London: Macmillan).

Hall, S. and Jefferson, T. (1989) (eds) *Resistance through Rituals: Youth Subcultures in Post-War Britain* (London: Unwin Hyman).

Harris, R. (1992) *Crime, Criminal Justice and the Probation Service* (London: Routledge).

Harris, R. and Webb, D. (1987) *Welfare, Power and Juvenile Justice* (London: Tavistock).

Harrison, B. (1992) 'Full-time Delinquents', *Police Review*, March 1992, pp. 484–5.

Hay, D. (1989) 'Prosecution and Power: Malicious Prosecution in the English Courts, 1750–1850' in D. Hay and F. Snyder (eds), *Policing and Prosecution in Britain 1750–1850* (Oxford: Clarendon Press).

Hay, D. and Snyder, F. (1989a) 'Using the Criminal Law, 1750–1850: Policing, Private Prosecution, and the State' in D. Hay and F. Snyder (eds), *Policing and Prosecution in Britain 1750–1850* (Oxford: Clarendon Press).

Hay, D. and Snyder, F. (1989b) (eds), *Policing and Prosecution in Britain 1750–1850* (Oxford: Clarendon Press).

Helsinki Institute for Crime Prevention and Control (HEUNI) (1986) *Non-Prosecution in Europe*. Report of the European Seminar held in Helsinki, Finland, 22–24 March 1986. Publication series no.9 (Helsinki: HEUNI).

Hewitt, M. and Pinchbeck, I. (1973) *Children in English Society* (London: Routledge & Kegan Paul).

Hilson, C. (1993) 'Discretion to Prosecute and Judicial Review', *Criminal Law Review*, October 1993, pp. 739–47.

Holdaway, S. (1986) 'Police and social work relations: problems and possibilities', *British Journal of Social Work*, vol. 16(2), pp. 137–60.

Home Affairs Committee, House of Commons (1993) *Sixth Report–Juvenile Offenders*, vol. 1 (London: HMSO).

Home Department (1879) *22nd Report of the Inspector of Reformatory and Industrial Schools.*

Home Department (1881) *Report to the Secretary of State for the Home Department on the State of the Law Relating to the Treatment and Punishment of Juvenile Offender.*

HM Chief Inspector of Constabulary (1978) *Report of Her Majesty's Chief Inspector of Constabulary 1977* (London: HMSO).

HM Chief Inspector of Constabulary (1979) *Report of Her Majesty's Chief Inspector of Constabulary 1978* (London: HMSO).

HM Government (1994) *Tackling Drugs Together – A Consultative Document Strategy for England 1995–1998* (London: HMSO).

HM Inspectorate of Probation (1993) *Annual Report 1992–93* (London: HMSO).

HM Inspectorate of Probation (1994) *Young Offenders and the Probation Service. Report of a Thematic Inspection* (London: HMSO).

Home Office (1923) *First Report on the Work of the Children's Branch.*

Home Office (1924) *Second Report on the Work of the Children's Branch.*

Home Office (1928) *Statistical Abstract for the U.K., No.72, 1913–1927.*

Home Office (1949) *Memorandum on Juvenile Delinquency, with Ministry of Education.*

Home Office (1951) *Sixth Report on the Work of the Children's Department.*

Home Office (1960) *Delinquent Generations. Studies in the Causes of Delinquency and the Treatment of Offenders*, vol. 3 (London: HMSO).

Home Office (1965) *The Child, the Family and the Young Offender*, Cmnd 2742 (London: HMSO).

Home Office (1968) *Children in Trouble*, Cmnd 3601 (London: HMSO).

Home Office (1970) *Guide to the 1969 Children and Young Persons Act* (London: HMSO).

Home Office (1974) *Young Adult Offenders* (London: HMSO).

Home Office (1976) *Children and Young Persons Act 1969: Observations on the 11th Report from the Expenditure Committee*, Cmnd 6494 (London: HMSO).

Home Office (1978) *The Cautioning of Offenders*, Circular 49/78 (London: HMSO).

Home Office (1980a) *Young Offenders*, Cmnd 8045 (London: HMSO).

Home Office (1981) *Criminal Statistics, England and Wales 1980*, Cmnd 8376 (London: HMSO).

Home Office (1984) *Cautioning by the Police: A Consultative Document* (London: HMSO).

Home Office (1985) *The Cautioning of Offenders*, Circular 14/85 (London: HMSO).
Home Office (1987) *Criminal Statistics, England and Wales 1986*, Cm 233 (London: HMSO).
Home Office (1988a) *Punishment, Custody and the Community*, Cm 424 (London: HMSO).
Home Office (1988b) *Tackling Offending: An Action Plan* (London: HMSO).
Home Office (1990a) *Crime, Justice and Protecting the Public*, Cm 965 (London: HMSO).
Home Office (1990b) *Partnership in Crime Prevention* (London: HMSO).
Home Office (1990c) *The Cautioning of Offenders*, Circular 59/1990 (London: HMSO).
Home Office (1990d) *Crime Prevention – the Success of the Partnership Approach* (London: HMSO).
Home Office (1990e) *Partnership in Dealing with Offenders in the Community. A Discussion Paper* (London: HMSO).
Home Office, Standing Conference on Crime Prevention (1991) *Safer Communities – the local delivery of crime prevention through the partnership approach (Morgan Report)* (London: HMSO).
Home Office (1992) *Criminal Statistics England and Wales 1990*, Cm 1935 (London: HMSO).
Home Office (1993) *Police Reform*, White Paper, Cm 2281 (London: HMSO).
Home Office (1994a) *The Cautioning of Offenders*, Circular 18/1994 (London: HMSO).
Home Office, Research and Statistics Department (1994b) *The Criminal Histories of Those Cautioned in 1985, 1988 and 1991*. Statistical Bulletin 94/8 (London: HMSO).
Home Office (1994c) *Criminal Statistics England and Wales 1993*, Cm 2680 (London: HMSO).
Home Office (1995a) *Strengthening Punishment in the Community*, Cm 2780 (London: HMSO).
Home Office (1995b) *National Standards for the Supervision of Offenders in the Community* (London: HMSO).
Home Office (1995c) *Criminal Statistics, England and Wales 1994*, Cm 3010 (London: HMSO).
Hope, T. and Shaw, M. (1988) (eds) *Communities and Crime Reduction* (London: HMSO).
Houghton, W. (1957) *The Victorian Frame of Mind 1830–1870* (New Haven: Yale University Press).
Hudson, B. (1987) *Justice through Punishment* (London: Macmillan).
Hughes, G., Leisten, R. and Pilkington, A. (1995) 'The Changing Organisation and Practice of Multi-Agency Diversion in Northamptonshire:

Some Current Research Findings'. Paper presented at the British Criminology Conference, University of Loughborough, July 1995.

Humphries, S. (1981) *Hooligans or Rebels? An Oral History of Working-Class Childhood and Youth 1889–1939* (Oxford: Basil Blackwell).

Humphry, D. and John, G. (1972) *Because They're Black* (Harmondsworth: Pelican).

Ignatieff, M. (1978) *A Just Measure of Pain: the Penitentiary in the Industrial Revolution 1750–1850* (London: Macmillan).

Ignatieff. M. (1979) 'Police and People', *New Society*, 30 August 1979, p. 445.

Ingleby Committee (1960) *Report of the Committee on Children and Young Persons*, Cmnd. 1191 (London: HMSO).

Institute for the Study of Labour and Economic Crisis (1982) *The Iron Fist and the Velvet Glove* (San Francisco: Crime and Social Justice Associates).

Jefferson, T. (1990) *The Case Against Paramilitary Policing* (Milton Keynes: Open University Press).

Johnston, L. (1992) *The Rebirth of Private Policing* (London: Macmillan).

Jones, C. (1993) 'Auditing Criminal Justice', *British Journal of Criminology*, vol. 33(3), pp. 187–202.

Jones, D. (1979) 'The Poacher: A Study in Victorian Crime and Protest', *Historical Journal*, XXII, p. 851.

Jones, D. (1982) *Crime, Protest, Community and Police in Nineteenth-Century Britain* (London: Routledge & Kegan Paul).

Jones, D.W. (1987) 'Recent development in work with young offenders', in J.C. Coleman (ed.), *Working with Troubled Adolescents* (London: Academic Press).

Jones, D.W. (1993) 'The successful revolution in juvenile justice continues – but for how long?', *Justice of the Peace*, 8 May 1993, pp. 297–8.

Jones, G. and Wallace, C. (1992) Youth, Family and Citizenship (Buckingham: Open University Press).

Jones, M. (1980) *Organisational Aspects of Police Behaviour* (Farnborough: Gower).

Judge, T. (1994) 'When I was a lad . . .' *Police*, XXVI (11), pp. 20–3.

The Justices' Clerks Society (1980) *Recommendations for Child Law Reform* (London: Justices' Clerk Society).

Keith, M. (1993) *Race, Riots and Policing. Lore and Disorder in a Multi-racist Society* (London: UCL Press).

Kelly, A. (1996) Introduction to the Scottish Children's Panel (Winchester: Waterside Press).

Kennedy, H. (1992) *Eve was Framed: Women and British Justice* (London: Chatto).

Kilbrandon Committee (1964) *Report of Committee on Children and Young Persons (Scotland)*, Cmnd 2306 (Edinburgh: HMSO).

King, R. (1991), 'Consultation: Panels or Bureaux?' Paper presented to a National Conference on Police Cautioning: Home Office Circular 59/1990. January 1991. Nottingham Polytechnic.

King, P. and Noel, (1993), 'The Origins of "The Problems of Juvenile Delinquency": The growth of Juvenile Prosecutions in London in the Late Eighteenth and Early nineteenth centuries', *Criminal Justice History*, pp. 17–41.

Kinsey, R. (1992) *Policing the City* (Edinburgh: Scottish Office).

Klein, M. (1979) 'Deinstitutionalization and diversion of juvenile offenders: a litany of impediments', in N. Morris and M. Tonry (eds), *Crime and Justice: an annual review of research*, vol. 1 (Chicago: University of Chicago Press).

Lacey, N. and Zedner, L. (1995) 'Discourses of Community in Criminal Justice', *Journal of Law and Society*, vol. 22(3), pp. 301–25.

Landau, S. (1981) 'Juveniles and the Police', *British Journal of Criminology*, vol. 21(1), pp. 27–46.

Landau, S. and Nathan, G. (1983) 'Selecting Delinquents for Cautioning in the London Metropolitan Area', *British Journal of Criminology*, vol. 23(2), pp. 128–49.

Laycock, G. and Tarling, R. (1984) 'Police Force Cautioning: Policy and Practice', in Home Office, *Cautioning by the Police: a Consultative Document* (London: Home Office).

Lee, J.A. (1981), 'Some structural aspects of police deviance in relations with minority groups' in C. Shearing (ed.), *Organizational Police Deviance* (Toronto: Butterworths).

Lee, M. (1994), 'The Probation Order: a suitable case for treatment?', *Drugs: education, prevention and policy*, vol. 1(2), pp. 121–33.

Lee, M. (1995), 'Across the Public-Private Divide? Private Policing, Grey Intelligence and Civil Actions in Local Drugs Control', *European Journal of Crime, Criminal Law and Criminal Justice*, vol. 3(4), pp. 381–94.

Lee, M. (1996), 'London: "Community Damage Limitation" through Policing?', in N. Dorn, J. Jepsen and E. Savona (eds), *European Drug Policies and Enforcement* (London: Macmillan).

Lemert, E. (1971) *Instead of Courts: diversion in juvenile justice* (Rockville, Md: National Institute of Mental Health).

Lemert, E. (1981) 'Diversion in Juvenile Justice: What Has Been Wrought', *Journal of Research in Crime and Delinquency*, vol. 18(1), pp. 34–46.

Leng, R. (1992) *The Right to Silence in Police Interrogation*, RCCJ Research Study No. 10 (London: HMSO).

Liverpool City Police (1952) *Report on the Liverpool City Police* (Liverpool: City Police).

Liverpool City Police (1962) *The Police and Children* (Liverpool: City Police).

Loader, I. (1996) *Youth, Policing and Democracy* (London: Macmillan).

Lock, J. (1979) *The British Policewoman* (London: Robert Hale).

Locke, T. (1990) *New Approaches to Crime in the 1990s* (London: Longman).

London Drug Policy Forum (1994) *Drugs and Community Safety: Promoting a Partnership Approach* (London: Metropolitan Police).

Longford Committee (1964) *Crime – a challenge to us all. Report of a Labour Party Study Group* (London: Labour Party).

Mack, J. (1963) 'Police Juvenile Liaison Schemes', *British Journal of Criminology*, vol. 3(4), pp. 361–75.

Macmillan, J. (1991) 'Social Information and Decision-Making in Juvenile Liaison Panels', in T. Booth (ed.), *Juvenile Justice in the New Europe* (Sheffield: Joint Unit for Social Services Research).

MacMillan, K. (1977) *Education Welfare: Strategy and Structure* (London: Longman).

Matthews, R. (1988) (ed.) *Informal Justice* (London: Sage).

Matthews, R. (1989) (ed.) *Privatizing Criminal Justice* (London: Sage).

Mawby, R. and Fisher, C. (1982) 'Social Work Influence on the Cautioning of Juvenile Offenders', *British Journal of Social Work*, vol. 12, pp. 471–86.

May, D. (1971) 'Delinquency Control and the Treatment Model: Some Implications of Recent Legislation', *British Journal of Criminology*, vol. 11(4), pp. 359–70.

May, M. (1973) 'Innocence and experience: the evolution of the concept of juvenile delinquency in the mid-nineteenth century', *Victorian Studies*, vol. 18(1), pp. 148–59.

May, T. (1991) *Probation: Politics, Policy and Practice* (Milton Keynes: Open University Press).

McCabe, S. and Wallington, P. with Alderson, T., Costin, L. and Mason, C. (1988) *The Police, Public Order and Civil Liberties: Legacies of the Miners' Strike* (London: Routledge).

McClintock, F.H. and Avison, N.H. (1968) *Crime in England and Wales.* Cambridge Studies in Criminology XXII (London: Heinemann).

McConville, M. and Hodgson, J. (1993) *Custodial Legal Advice and the Right to Silence.* The Royal Commission on Criminal Justice Research Study No.16 (London: HMSO).

McConville, M., Sanders, A. and Leng, R. (1991) *The Case for the Prosecution* (London: Routledge).

McKenzie, I. (1995) 'A Clip Round the Ear', *Policing*, vol. 11(3), pp. 194–202.

McKittrick, N. and Eysenck, S. (1984) 'Diversion: a big fix?', *Justice of the Peace*, 23 June, pp. 377–9 and pp. 393–4.

McLaughlin, E. and Muncie, J. (1993) 'Juvenile Delinquency', in R. Dallas and E. McLaughlin (eds), *Social Problems and the Family* (London: Sage).

McLaughlin, E. (1994) *Community, Policing and Accountability* (Aldershot: Avebury).

McLaughlin, E. (1996) 'Police, Policing and Policework' in E. McLaughlin and J. Muncie (eds), *Controlling Crime* (London: Sage).

McLaughlin, E. and Muncie, J. (1994) 'Managing the Criminal Justice System' in J. Clarke, A. Cochrane and E. McLaughlin (eds), *Managing Social Policy* (London: Sage).

McLaughlin, E. and Muncie, J. (eds) (1996) *Controlling Crime* (London: Sage).

McWilliams, W. (1987) 'Probation, pragmatism and policy', *Howard Journal of Criminal Justice*, vol. 26(2), pp. 97–121.

Menter, I. (1987) 'The long arm of education: a review of recent documents on police/school liaison', *Critical Social Policy*, vol. 21, pp. 68–77.

Miller, W.R. (1977) 'Never on Sunday', in D.Bayley (ed.), *Police and Society*.

Molony Committee (1927) *Report of the Departmental Committee on the Treatment of Young Offenders*, Cmd. 2831.

Morris, A. (1974) 'Scottish Juvenile Justice: a Critique' in R. Hood (ed.), *Crime, Criminology and Public Policy* (London: Heinemann).

Morris, A. (1978) 'Diversion of Juvenile Offenders from the Criminal Justice System', in N. Tutt (ed.), *Alternative Strategies for Coping with Crime* (Oxford: Blackwell).

Morris, A. (1987) *Women, Crime and Criminal Justice* (Oxford: Basil Blackwell).

Morris, A. and Giller, H. (1977) 'The Juvenile Court – the Client's Perspective', *Criminal Law Review*, pp. 198–205.

Morris, A. and Giller, H. (eds) (1983) *Providing Criminal Justice for Children* (London: Edward Arnold).

Morris, A., Giller, H., Szwed, E., and Geach, H. (1980) *Justice for Children* (London: Macmillan).

Morris, A. and McIsaac, M. (1978) *Juvenile Justice?* (London: Heinemann).

Mott, J. (1983) 'Police decisions for dealing with juvenile offenders', *British Journal of Criminology*, vol. 23(3), pp. 249–62.

Moxon, D. (1985) *Managing Criminal Justice* (London: HMSO).

Muncie, J. (1984) *The trouble with kids today: youth and crime in postwar Britain* (London: Hutchison).

Muncie, J. and McLaughlin, E. (eds) (1996) *The Problem of Crime* (London: Sage).

NACRO (1989) *Diverting Juvenile Offenders from Prosecution* (London: NACRO).

NACRO (1991a) *Black People and the Criminal Justice System* (London: NACRO).

NACRO (1991b) *Race and Criminal Justice*. NACRO Briefing (London: NACRO).

NACRO (1992) *Diverting Young Offenders from Prosecution* (London: NACRO).

NACRO (1993) *Community Provision for Young People in the Youth Justice System – A Survey of Local Authorities*. NACRO Young Offenders Committee Occasional Paper 2 (London: NACRO).

NACRO (1994) *Partnership with Parents in Dealing with Young Offenders*, NACRO Young Offenders Committee Policy Paper 4 (London: NACRO).

NAPO (1981) *The provision of alternatives to custody and the use of the use of the probation order* (London: NAPO).

National Audit Office (1991) *Promoting Value for Money in Provincial Police Forces* (London: HMSO).

National Youth Agency (1991) *Parental Involvement in Intermediate Treatment* (Leicester: NYA).

National Youth Bureau (1979) *How Much I.T.?* National Youth Bureau fact sheet. (Leicester: National Youth Bureau).

Nellis, M. (1989) 'Juvenile Justice and the Voluntary Sector', in R. Matthews (ed.), *Privatizing Criminal Justice* (London: Sage).

Northamptonshire County Council, Juvenile Liaison Bureaux (1985) *Statement on Philosophy, Objectives and Operation*. Northamptonshire County Council.

O'Dowd, D., Atkinson, J., Woodward, D. and Blackham, P. (1991) 'Pre-court decision-making in juvenile justice: some comments', *British Journal of Criminology*, vol. 31(2), pp. 189–91.

Odgers, F. (1954) 'Prevention of Juvenile Crime', *Criminal Law Review*, pp. 173–5.

Oliver, I. (1973) 'The Metropolitan Police Juvenile Bureaux Scheme', *Criminal Law Review*, pp. 499–506.

Oliver, I. (1978) *The Metropolitan Police Approach to the Prosecution of Juvenile Offenders* (London: Peel Press).

Page R. and Clark, G. (1977) *Who Cares? Young People in Care Speak Out* (London: National Children's Bureau).

Paley, J. and Thorpe, D. (1974) *Children: handle with care* (Leicester: National Youth Bureau).

Parker, H. (1974) *The View from the Boys* (Newton Abbot: David & Charles).

Parker, H., Casburn, M. and Turnbull, D. (1981) *Receiving Juvenile Justice* (Oxford: Basil Blackwell).

Parker, H., Sumner, M. and Jarvis, G. (1989) *Unmasking the Magistrates* (Milton Keynes: Open University Press).

Parliamentary All-Party Penal Affairs Group (1981) *Young Offenders – a Strategy for the Future* (Chichester: Barry Rose).

Parry, N. and Parry, J. (1979) 'Social work, professionalism and the state', in N. Parry, M. Rustin and C. Satyamurti (eds), *Social Work, Welfare and the State* (London: Edward Arnold).

Patchett, K. and McClean, L. (1965) 'Decision-making in juvenile cases', *Criminal Law Review*, pp. 699–710.

Paterson, F. (1989) *Out of Place: Public Policy and the Emergence of Truancy* (London: Falmer Press).

Pearson, G. (1983) *Hooligan: A history of respectable fears* (London: Macmillan).

Pearson, G., Blagg, H., Smith, D., Sampson, A. and Stubbs, P. (1992) 'Crime community and conflict: the multi-agency approach', in D. Downes (ed.), *Unravelling Criminal Justice* (London: Macmillan).

Pellew, J. (1982) *The Home Office 1848–1914: from clerks to bureaucrats* (London: Heinemann Educational).

Petrow, S. (1994) *Policing Morals – the Metropolitan Police and the Home Office 1870–1914* (Oxford: Clarendon Press).

Philips, S., and Cochrane, R. (1988) *The Role and Function of Police Community Liaison Officers*. Home Office Research and Planning Unit Paper 51 (London: HMSO).

Phillips, D. (1980) ' "A New Engine of Power and Authority": the institutionalization of law enforcement in England 1780–1830', in V. Gatrell, B. Lenman and G. Parker (eds), *Crime and the Law* (London: Europa).

Philp, A.F. and Timms, N. (1957) *The Problem of the 'Problem Family'* (London: Family Service Units).

Pitts, J. (1988) *The Politics of Juvenile Crime* (London: Sage).

Platt, A. (1969) *The Child Savers* (Chicago: University Press).

Pratt, J. (1986) 'Diversion from the Juvenile Court', *British Journal of Criminology*, vol. 26(3), pp. 212–33.

Pratt, J. (1989) 'Corporatism: the Third Model of Juvenile Justice', *British Journal of Criminology*, vol. 29(3), pp. 236–54.

The President's Commission on Law Enforcement and Administration of Justice, Task Force on Juvenile Delinquency (1967) *Juvenile Delinquency and Youth Crime* (Washington DC: US Government Printing Office).

Raffe, D. (1991) 'The transition from school to work: context, content and the external labour market', in C. Wallace and M. Cross (eds) *Youth in Transition* (Basingstoke: Falmer Press).

Rainton, D. (1974) 'Police discretion: a study of how it works in Sussex', *Police Review* 12 July, pp. 878–9 (Part I), 19 July, pp. 912–13 (Part II), and 26 July, pp. 945–50 (Part III).

Ralphs, R. (1986) 'The evolution of control', *Justice of the Peace*, pp. 154–6.

Reid, K. and Kendall, L. (1982) 'A review of some recent research into persistent school absenteeism', *British Journal of Education Studies*, vol. 30(3), pp. 295–312.

Reiner, R. (1985) *The Politics of the Police* (Brighton: Wheatsheaf).

Reiner, R. (1994) 'Policing and the Police', in M. Maguire, R. Morgan and R. Reiner (eds), *Oxford Handbook of Criminology* (Oxford: Clarendon Press).

Richardson, N. (1989) *Justice By Geography III – legislation, demography and decision-making* (Manchester: Social Information Systems).

Richardson, N. (1990) 'A decade of diversion', *Social Work Today*, vol. 21(23), pp. 24–5.

Ritchie, M. and Mack, J. (1974) *Police Warnings* (Glasgow: University Press).

Rose, D. (1992) *Climate of Fear* (London: Bloomsbury).

Rose, G. and Hamilton, R. (1970) 'Effects of a Juvenile Liaison Scheme', *British Journal of Criminology*, vol. 10(1), pp. 2–20.

Rose, N. (1990) *Governing the Soul – the Shaping of the Private Self* (London: Routledge).

Royal Commission on Criminal Procedure (1981) *The investigation and prosecution of criminal offences in England and Wales: the law and procedure*, Cmnd 8092–1 (London: HMSO).

Royal Commission on Criminal Justice (1993) *Report*, Cm 2263 (London: HMSO).

Rutherford, A. (1992) *Growing Out of Crime – The New Era* (Winchester: Waterside Press).

Rutter, M. and Giller, H. (1983) *Juvenile Delinquency: Trends and Perspectives* (Harmondsworth: Penguin).

Sampson, A., Stubbs, P., Smith, D., Pearson, G. and Blagg, H. (1988) 'Crime, Localities and the Multi-Agency Approach', *British Journal of Criminology*, vol. 28(4), pp. 478–93.

Sandell, G. (1992) 'Appropriate behaviour', *Community Case*, 25 June, pp. 18–19.

Sanders, A. (1985a) 'Class Bias in Prosecutions', *Howard Journal of Criminal Justice*, vol. 24, pp. 76–99.

Sanders, A. (1985b) 'Prosecution Decisions and the Attorney-General's Guidelines', *Criminal Law Review*, pp. 4–19.

Sanders, A. (1986) 'Diverting Offenders from Prosecution: What can we learn from other countries?', *Justice of the Peace*, September 1986, pp. 614–17.

Sanders, A. (1988) 'The Limits to Diversion from Prosecution', *British Journal of Criminology*, vol. 28(4), pp. 513–32.

Sanders, A. (1994), 'From Suspect to Trial', M. Maguire et al. (eds), *The Oxford Handbook of Criminology* (Oxford: Clarendon Press).

Sanders, A. and Bridges, L. (1990) 'Access to Legal Advice and Police Malpractice', *Criminal Law Review*, July 1990, pp. 494–509.

Sanders, A. and Young, R. (1994) *Criminal Justice* (London: Butterworth).

Sarri, R. (1983) 'Paradigms and pitfalls in juvenile justice diversion', in A. Morris and H. Giller (eds), *Providing Criminal Justice for Children* (London: Edward Arnold).

Schaffer, E. (1980) *Community Policing* (London: Croom Helm).

Schur, E. (1973) *Radical Non-intervention: Rethinking the Delinquency Problem* (Englewood Cliffs, NJ: Prentice-Hall).

Scraton, P. (1985) *The State of the Police* (London: Pluto).

Scraton, P. (1987) (ed.) *Law, Order and the Authoritarian State* (Milton Keynes: Open University Press).

Scull, A. (1977) *Decarceration: Community Treatment and the Deviant – a Radical View* (Englewood Cliffs, NJ: Prentice-Hall).

Sebba, L. (1967) 'Decision-making in juvenile cases – a comment', *Criminal Law Review*, pp. 347–55.

Sharpe, J. (1984) *Crime in Early Modern England 1550–1750* (London: Longman).

Smellie, E. and Crow, I. (1991) *Black People's Experience of Criminal Justice* (London: NACRO).

Smith, D. and Gray, J. (1983) *Police and People in London: the Police in Action, Volume 4* (London: Policy Studies Institute).

Smith, D., Paylor, I. and Mitchell, P. (1993) 'Partnerships Between the Independent Sector and the Probation Service', *Howard Journal of Criminal Justice*, vol. 32(1), pp. 25–39.

Smith, P. (1985) *Policing Victorian London. Political Policing, Public Order, and the London Metropolitan Police* (Westport: Greenwood Press).

Smith, T. (1985) 'Law talk: juveniles' understanding of legal language', *Journal of Criminal Justice*, vol. 13(4), pp. 339–53.

Smithies, E. (1982) *Crime in Wartime: a Social History of crime in World War II* (London: Allen & Unwin).

Somerville, J. (1969) 'A study of the preventive aspect of police work with juveniles', *Criminal Law Review*, pp. 407–14.

Steer, D. (1970) *Police Cautioning – a Study in the Exercise of Police Discretion*, Oxford University Penal Research Unit (Oxford: Basil Blackwell).

Storch, R. (1975) 'The plague of the blue locusts: police reform and popular resistance in northern England 1840–57', *International Review of Social History*, vol. 20, pp. 61–90.

Storch, R. (1976) 'The Policeman as Domestic Missionary: Urban Discipline and Popular Culture in Northern England, 1850–1880', *Journal of Social History*, vol. 9, pp. 481–509.

Stubbs, P. (1988) 'Relationships with the Police: Intermediate Treatment and the Multi-Agency Approach', *Youth and Policy*, vol. 24, pp. 16–19.

Taylor, M. (1971) *Study of the Juvenile Liaison Scheme in West Ham 1961–1965*. Home Office Research Unit Report No.8 (London: HMSO).

Thomas, T. (1988) 'The Police and Criminal Evidence Act 1984: the Social Work Role', *Howard Journal of Criminal Justice*, vol. 27(4), pp. 256–65.

Thorpe, D. (1978) 'Intermediate Treatment' in N. Tutt (eds), *Alternative Strategies for Coping with Crime* (Oxford: Blackwell).

Thorpe, D. (1983) 'De-institutionalization and justice', in A. Morris and H. Giller (eds), *Providing Criminal Justice for Children* (London: Edward Arnold).

Thorpe, D. (1994) 'Police and Juvenile Offending', M. Stephens and S. Becker (eds), *Police Force, Police Service – Care and Control in Britain* (London: Macmillan).

Thorpe, D., Smith, D., Green, C. and Paley, J. (1980) *Out of Care: the community support of juvenile offenders* (London: George Allen & Unwin).

Timms, N. (1964) *Development of Psychiatric Social Work in Great Britain 1939–1962* (London: Routledge & Kegan Paul).

Tobias, J.J. (1967) *Crime and Industrial Society in the Nineteenth Century* (London: Batsford).

Tutt, N. (ed.) (1978) *Alternative Strategies for Coping with Crime* (Oxford: Blackwell and Robertson).

Tutt, N. and Giller, H. (1983) 'Police Cautioning of Juveniles: the Practice of Diversity', *Criminal Law Review*, pp. 587–95.

Tutt, N. and Giller, H. (1984) *Diversion* (Lancaster: Lancaster Information Systems).

Tutt, N. and Giller, H. (1987) 'Manifesto for Management – the Elimination of Custody', *Justice of the Peace*, pp. 200–2.

Vass, A. (1990) *Alternatives to Prison* (London: Sage).

Walker, M. (1987) 'Interpreting race and crime statistics', *Journal of the Royal Statistical Society*, Series A, vol. 150(1), pp. 39–56.

Walker, M., Jefferson, T. and Senevirate, M. (1989) 'Race and criminal justice in a provincial city', unpublished paper presented to British Criminology Conference, Bristol Polytechnic, July.

Wardhaugh, J. (1990) 'Regulating truancy: the role of the Education Welfare Service', *Sociological Review*, vol. 38(4), pp. 735–64.

Wardhaugh, J. (1991) 'Criminalising Truancy: Legal and Welfare Responses to School Non-Attendance', T. Booth (ed.), *Juvenile Justice in the New Europe* (Sheffield: Joint Unit for Social Services Research).

Wasik, M. and von Hirsch, A. (1988) 'Non-custodial penalties and the principles of desert', *Criminal Law Review*, pp. 555–72.

Watson, J. (1942) *The Child and the Magistrate* (London: Jonathan Cape).

Weinberger, B. (1981) 'The Police and the Public in Mid-Nineteenth Century Warwickshire', in V. Bailey (ed.), *Policing and Punishment*.

Weinberger, B. (1995) *The Best Police in the World* (Aldershot: Scolar Press).

Westwood, D. (1991a) 'The Effects of Home Office Guidelines on the Cautioning of Offenders', *Criminal Law Review*, pp. 591–7.

Westwood, D. (1991b) 'The "Justice" Approach: a Working Model'. Paper presented to a National Conference on Police Cautioning: Home Office Circular 59/1990. January 1991. Nottingham Polytechnic.

White, J. (1986) *The Worst Street in North London: Campbell Bunk, Islington, between the wars* (London: Routledge & Kegan Paul).

Widdowson, B. (1989) 'Cautioning or Excusing', *Justice of the Peace*, pp. 168–9.

Wilkinson, C. and Evans, R. (1990a), 'Police Cautioning of Juveniles: the Impact of Home Office Circular 14/1985', *Criminal Law Review*, pp. 165–76.

Wilkinson, C. and Evans, R. (1990b) 'Variations in Police Cautioning Policy and Practice in England and Wales', *Howard Journal of Criminal Justice*, vol. 29(3), pp. 155–76.

Williams, C. (1954) 'Turning a Blind Eye', *Criminal Law Review*, pp. 271–3.

Williamson, H. (1993) 'Youth policy in the United Kingdom and the marginalisation of young people', *Youth and Policy*, issue 40, pp. 33–48.

Willis, C. (1983) *The Use, Effectiveness and Impact of Police Stop and Search Powers* (London: HMSO).

Woolf, Lord Justice (1991) *Prison Disturbances, April 1990* (London: HMSO).

Worrall, A. (1990) *Offending Women: Female Lawbreakers and the Criminal Justice System* (London: Routledge).

Wright, A. (1993) 'Towards an appropriate model of diversion from the criminal court process', *Justice of the Peace*, pp. 184–6.

Zander, M. (1975) *Diversion from criminal justice in an English context: Report of a NACRO Working Party* (Chichester: Barry Rose).

Index